The Wallpapering Book

Julian Cassell & Peter Parham

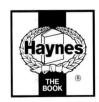

Haynes

THE BOOK ®

Contents

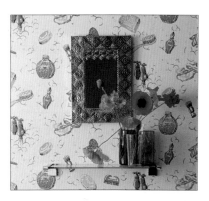

Wallpapering 50

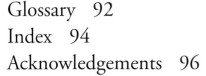

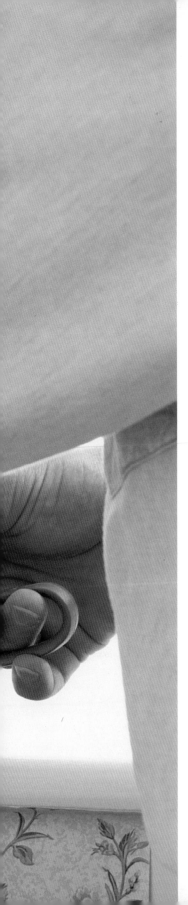

Introduction

Wallpaper can be one of the most dramatic and instant ways of transforming the home. These days, as never before, there is an almost unlimited variety from which to choose, from classical elegance to striking modern statements.

Some people believe that wallpapering is difficult, but with this book it is no longer daunting. To start, 'Ideas and Choices' will help form your decorative ideas, and allow you to marry them up with the practical function of each room in the house.

The old adage of 'preparation is everything' still rings true, so 'Planning and Preparation' takes you from a shopping list of all the tools and materials you may require through to preparing a sound surface. By following the 'Lining' steps you can make all the difference to achieving a superior finish, and they will also give you invaluable practice before hanging your chosen wallpaper.

'Wallpapering' covers every facet of hanging paper, from where to start, through awkward joins and obstacles, to helping you solve any problems along the way. Whether you are an 'old hand' or a novice at papering, you will learn both the easiest and correct way of tackling each task.

Although there is much work ahead of you, we hope that this book will help you to enjoy doing it, and that the results will give pleasure for many years to come.

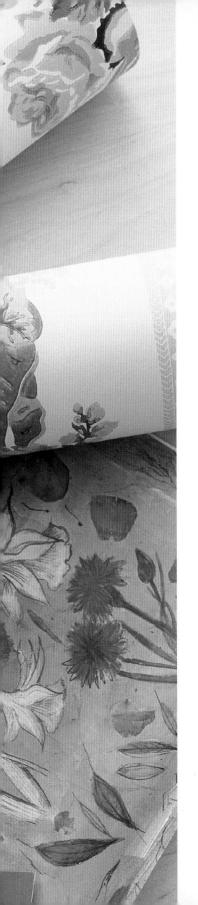

Ideas and Choices

Making a decision on wallpaper design and pattern is often a difficult process, especially when trying to match the paper with paint colours, furnishings and carpets. Personal tastes vary dramatically, so try not to be influenced too much by the experts who sometimes get a little carried away with using particular wall coverings in specific areas of the home. Remember that it is your choice that counts.

This chapter offers simple advice on the visual effects of the various types of wallpaper available. There are also guidelines on the practicality of particular papers and which rooms they are most suited to. For example, some may be best used in a kitchen or bathroom rather than a lounge.

It is helpful to use all available props to assist you to make the right decision. Browsing through magazines, trying to determine your favourite colours and using samples of wallpaper can all aid the process and achieve a finished product that has been worth the work involved.

Colour schemes and designs

The predominant colour of wallpaper obviously affects the atmosphere of a room. Warm colours, such as oranges or yellows, 'advance' to create a welcoming atmosphere, while cooler colours, such as greens or blues, create an impression of space and a fresh, soothing mood. Many wallpaper designs contain a number of different colours and it can be difficult to decide which is the dominant colour. In such cases, the bolder, darker colours tend to be the decisive influence.

Pattern size needs equal consideration. Large patterns tend to be the most dramatic, whereas 'busy' patterns are excellent for disguising imperfections and are generally easier for the beginner to hang, as small mistakes in paper-hanging technique are lost in the energetic design. Symmetrical papers, such as stripes, must be applied very precisely, as they tend to accentuate any faults.

◀ Large floral designs are classic decorative wallpaper patterns. Always take into account room size when using them as they can be overpowering in a small area. In rooms that are predominantly used for relaxing, large floral patterns will always give a feeling of luxury and elegance.

◀ Smaller, repetitive designs create a more active impression within a room. They help to hide imperfections, both in the wall and in paper-hanging skills, and provide excellent backdrops for paintings, ornaments and general architectural features.

▶ Wallpaper should always be complemented by the other colours in the room. Choose the colours of paint for woodwork carefully and always try out test patches of the paint and wallpaper before purchasing large quantities and going ahead with the decoration. Once the basic colour scheme has been selected, consider amalgamating suitable wallpaper with decorative paint effects, such as the marbled wood panels shown here.

Creating a mood

The choice of wallpaper can be heavily influenced by the sort of mood that is required. For example, great sense of formality may be conveyed by stripes, or a country cottage effect may be created by using a small floral pattern.

Careful consideration of other features, such as the period of the house, how to highlight furnishings and simply what the room is actually used for, should all influence the decisions made.

Remember that people spend more time in some rooms at particular times of the day. For example, it is best to view a sample of wallpaper for the bedroom under artificial lighting, whereas for the kitchen, viewing under natural light is more sensible.

◄ In more intimate rooms, there is huge scope for allowing your most personal tastes to flourish. Although you should never be influenced by 'what people might think', most people are inevitably inhibited by others' opinions. However, in the privacy of your own bedroom, there is ample opportunity to be daring.

▶ Borders provide another decorative option and produce a stunning effect when dividing two different types of wallpaper. Many papers are designed to be over-painted, such as the embossed paper featured below the dado rail.

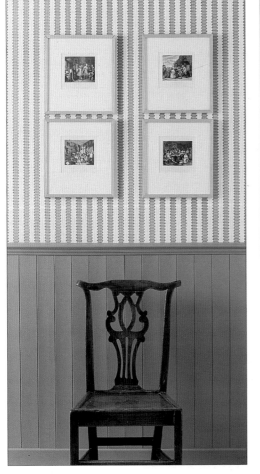

◀ Wallpaper stripes always create a sense of order, often with a traditional feel. It is particularly effective to use striped paper in conjunction with a complementary patterned paper or, as shown here, with a matching paint finish below a dado rail.

Practical papering

When selecting wallpaper, it is important to bear in mind the practicality of the paper for the room it is decorating. Some wallpapers are particularly delicate and should therefore not be used in areas where hard-wearing characteristics are required. The different types of paper 'finish' are discussed and illustrated more comprehensively on pages 14–15, but the examples below offer suggestions on ideal areas of use for wallpapers with different properties.

◀ Bathrooms are prone to high levels of condensation and a moist atmosphere. A vinyl paper is ideal to use here as its washable – or sometimes even scrubbable – coating protects it from the damp and keeps it easy to clean. A practical paper need not be a boring one; the choice is always huge.

◄ Children's rooms can be great fun to decorate, and give licence to all sorts of experimentation. As well as being decorative, borders divide the walls into upper and lower sections. The beauty of using them in this way is because children will tend to damage lower areas more than the higher ones. It is easier to redecorate regularly below the border rather than having to do the whole room just because the bottom section has been damaged.

▼ A kitchen is another area of the home that requires continual wiping down and general cleaning. A relief paper produces a durable decorative surface which can be painted in bold colours to enhance its texture, or in paler tones to give classical elegance. Again, a border is used to complement the wallpaper design.

Wallpaper finishes

Wall coverings can have various types of finish to suit different purposes. Some are more hard wearing than others, whereas some make decorative effects their main priority.

The most common categories of wallpaper are illustrated below, but there are various proprietary papers available that have slightly different characteristics again. Always be sure to check the manufacturer's guidelines before hanging such papers, in order to determine their suitability.

Lining

Flat undecorated paper hung on bare wall surfaces prior to decorative wallpaper.

Standard pattern

Flat wallpaper that has had a coloured design machine printed on to its surface.

Woodchip

Consists of two layers of paper bonded together with small chips of wood sealed between them. It provides a textured finish that is excellent for disguising rough wall surfaces. It should be painted after application, when thoroughly dried out.

BORDERS

Decorative bands of wallpaper are available in various finishes. They are generally applied horizontally at ceiling or dado level, but other uses are possible.

WALLPAPER SYMBOLS

When choosing paper check the label symbols for factors such as washability, hanging method and pattern match.

Vinyl

Popular, mass-produced vinyl papers come in a huge variety of patterns. Consist of a clear vinyl layer bonded on top of a printed pattern. Easy to keep clean and ideal in areas that need frequent cleaning. Heavy-duty vinyls are ideal for kitchens and bathrooms.

Heavy-duty vinyl

A thick and very hard-wearing vinyl paper, particularly useful for areas such as kitchens and bathrooms that get damp and need constant cleaning. As it is so heavy, a strong adhesive is required or it is likely to peel off the wall.

Blown vinyl

Similar to ordinary vinyl except a relief pattern is mounted on the flat backing paper, producing a textured finish. The relief pattern tends to be solid or compressible and is therefore more hard-wearing than that on embossed papers (see below).

Hand-printed

There are two main categories: screen printed or block printed. Both are printed one roll at a time. Pattern matching is often difficult and edges may need trimming before hanging. Usually expensive but the overall effect can be stunning.

Embossed

A relief pattern is imprinted in the paper during manufacture, producing a raised decorative surface. Some are white and are usually painted once hung, while others are already decorated. Take care not to flatten the relief during application.

Flock

Decorated with a pattern that has been cut into fibres built into the surface. Originally these were made from silk or wool, but today synthetic equivalents are more common and easier to hang. The pattern is mounted on flat backing paper.

Planning and Preparation

For wallpapering to be successful, it is essential to plan and prepare thoroughly for every step. Making decisions about materials and tools required, and about exactly how to go about the job, are crucial to the whole project running smoothly. All wallpaper – whatever the price or quality – requires a sound and well-prepared surface on which to hang, so the hard work of preparation is just as important as the actual paper hanging itself. Therefore, working carefully at this vital stage will make sure of a first rate finish that will last for a long time.

This chapter contains

Tools

When choosing and purchasing tools and equipment, always opt for quality rather than quantity. A few well-selected, superior items will be far more useful than many cheaper, inferior ones.

When assembling tools, it is not necessary to purchase the complete range listed here. Instead, buy for your specific needs and build up your equipment gradually. Also, if you have limited use for an item, especially a more expensive one such as a steam stripper, it may be more sensible to consider hiring it rather than buying.

BASIC TOOLBOX FOR PREPARATION

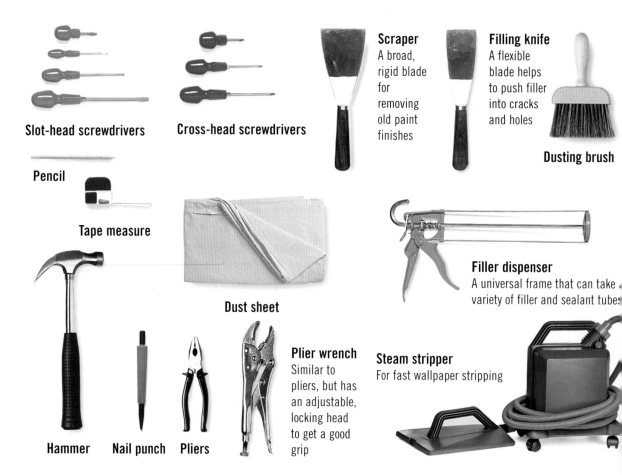

Slot-head screwdrivers

Cross-head screwdrivers

Scraper
A broad, rigid blade for removing old paint finishes

Filling knife
A flexible blade helps to push filler into cracks and holes

Dusting brush

Pencil

Tape measure

Dust sheet

Filler dispenser
A universal frame that can take a variety of filler and sealant tubes

Hammer **Nail punch** **Pliers**

Plier wrench
Similar to pliers, but has an adjustable, locking head to get a good grip

Steam stripper
For fast wallpaper stripping

Access and working surfaces

Trestles and plank
Make a sturdy platform when working on ceilings or high walls

Step-ladder

Pasting table

Personal protection

Protective gloves
Waterproof, to keep irritants off hands

Goggles
Keep dust, spray and chemicals out of eyes

Dust masks
(disposable)

WALLPAPERING TOOLS

Paper-hanging scissors

Craft knife

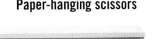

Wallpaper trough

Craft knife with snap-off blades

Bucket   **Stirring stick**   **Sponge**   **Measuring jug**

Spirit level

Steel rule

Plumb line
Indicates an exact vertical

Chalk line
Marks a long, straight line where distance is too long for a steel rule

Seam roller
Presses joins flat, when hanging paper

Fitch
For adding paste

Pasting brush

Radiator roller

Paper-hanging brush

Identifying problems

Before starting any preparation, the room must first be cleared of obstacles. It is best to remove all the furniture, accessories and soft furnishings and to take up the carpet now, if it is to be replaced. If it is not possible to totally clear the room, place everything in the middle and cover with dust sheets. You are now able to get a clear view of any problem areas, decide how to treat them and to assess the extent of redecoration required.

If any painting is needed, this must be carried out before you hang the wallpaper. As a general order of work you should prepare all surfaces, line ceilings and walls if necesssary, carry out any painting, and then finally hang your wallpaper. It is a lot easier to wipe excess paste off a painted surface rather than clean paint splashes off an expensive wall covering.

The problems outlined below are commonplace in many homes. All of them need attention before any work is carried out.

DAMP AND MOULD

Mould is caused by a build-up of moisture, normally as a result of poor ventilation. Wash it down with fungicide. Extensive mould growth should be looked at by a professional as there may be a general damp problem that needs to be solved before redecoration. Old stains, caused by damp that has now dried out, can be covered with proprietary sealers.

CRACKS IN PLASTER

Cracks are caused by walls drying out, by settlement or slight subsidence of the building, and by general wear and tear. Fill with an all-purpose filler and allow them to dry out completely before papering the wall (see pages 26–27).

POWDERY WALL SURFACES

Found in older houses previously painted with distemper, or may just be due to the breakdown of plaster due to age. Wash down and seal (see pages 28–29).

EFFLORESCENCE

This fluffy, grainy texture found on walls both old and new results from crystallisation of salts found in building materials. Use a scraper to remove deposits until no more appear.

FLAKY PAINT

Caused by moisture under paint, or where paint has been unable to stick to a powdery or incompatible surface. (See Damp and Mould, page 20, and Powdery Wall Surfaces, left.)

FLAKING TEXTURED FINISHES

Caused by water penetration (such as a leaking water pipe) or a poorly prepared wall surface. All textured finishes must be removed before papering can take place.

UNEVEN PAPERED SURFACES

Generally found in older properties. If the paper is basically sound or an overall 'rustic' finish is acceptable, do not strip as the plaster underneath may come away from the wall.

WRINKLED LINING PAPER

Found in corners where the walls are not square and poor adhesion plus slight building shift has lifted and torn paper. Small areas can be cut out with a scraper, and filled, before papering.

BUBBLING PAPER

Bubbles are inevitably caused by inexpert papering or poor adhesion to the wall. Strip all the paper (see pages 24–25) before hanging lining paper and new wall covering.

LIFTING SEAMS

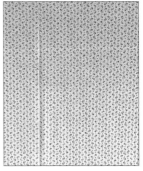

Due to lack of paste adhesion. Small areas of lining paper can be stuck back down with border adhesive prior to wallpapering. If it occurs with wallpaper it must be stripped.

Paper and materials

Wallpaper is the most expensive item on your shopping list, so just take care when calculating the number of rolls needed. However it is not just wallpaper that is needed to complete the job, so the check-list below may help when working out your requirements, depending on the particular wall covering you have chosen.

As with tools, remember that inferior materials may not be user-friendly. Buying good-quality products may cost extra, but will be money well spent.

BASIC SUPPLIES
Fillers

All-purpose filler
For holes and cracks

Ready-mixed filler

Flexible filler
For joints and cracks where movement is likely

Stripping, sanding and sizing

Sanding block
Sandpaper already attached to a supporting block

Stripping tablets
Help to strip wallpaper

Sugar soap
Cleans walls prior to painting

Sandpaper
Fine, medium and coarse grades

Spray-on stain block

PVA adhesive
For sealing surfaces before painting or papering

Size
Makes walls less absorbent and papering easier

Craft-knife blades
Replace often for a sharp edge at all times

Stockinette roll

Paper hanging

Overlap adhesive
Stronger than ordinary paste

Wallpaper paste

Ready-mixed paste

Border adhesive

PAPERS

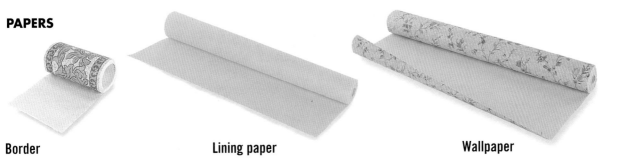

Border   **Lining paper**   **Wallpaper**

MEASURING UP

First, you must think about pattern repeats (see page 54). Papers with a large repeat pattern tend to produce more waste than when using a paper with a small repeat pattern.

To find out how many rolls of wallpaper are needed, calculate the total area to be papered: see the diagram to the right, which illustrates the easiest method.

1 Measure these two lengths and multiply together to calculate the area of the ceiling.

2 Measure these two lengths and multiply them together to calculate the area of the wall to the right of the chimney breast. Use the same technique to work out the area of all other walls. Do not deduct anything for obstacles such as doors and windows, as you will need to compensate for wastage when trimming during application of the paper.

3 For wallpapering with patterned paper, add on the size of the repeat pattern to the height of the room when calculating surface area. This will allow for unavoidable wastage when applying the paper.

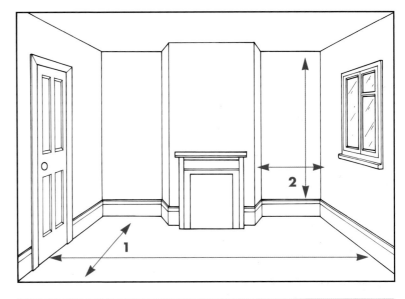

ROLLS OF WALLPAPER NEEDED

Total Surface Area to Paper		No of rolls	
sq m	sq yd		
5	6	1	For every additional
10	12	2	5sq m (6sq yd), add
15	18	3	one roll of wallpaper.

Standard rolls of wallpaper are approximately 52cm x 10m = 5.2sq m (20½in x 11yd = 6¼sq yd). The excess of 0.2sq m (¼sq yd) per roll allows for both trimming and wastage.

If you are not using standard rolls, simply work out the surface area of the rolls you are using and create your own table by the same method as above.

Stripping paper

This is a time-consuming job, but with the correct methods it is reasonably straightforward. A steam stripper, which can be hired quite cheaply, speeds up the process. When using it, always wear rubber gloves and goggles as boiling water and steam can spit out from the sides of the stripping pad. If a steam stripper is not available, soak the paper with hot water or use a stripping-tablet solution instead. Gloves and goggles are still required as most stripping chemicals will irritate the skin.

TOOLS: Gloves, goggles, steam stripper, scraper, measuring jug, bucket, stirring stick, 130mm (5in) brush, wallpaper spiker/ orbital scorer

MATERIALS: Stripping tablets, hot water

STEAM STRIPPING

1 When using a steam stripper always read the instructions. Check that the steam stripper is turned off at its power source, then pour water into its reservoir. Warm water will reduce the time needed for the stripper to boil. Then switch on the power and wait for the water to boil. Never leave a steam stripper unattended when it is switched on.

2 Put on your goggles and gloves. Place the stripper's steam pad firmly on the wallpaper you wish to strip, and hold it in the same position, without moving, for about 30 seconds. Some brands of wallpaper stripper, and some heavyweight papers, may require a longer time for steaming.

3 Move the pad across the wall and using a scraper, strip off the loose, bubbling paper. Take care not to dig the end of the scraper into the wall, gouging holes in the plaster. You will soon build up a rhythm of stripping the paper with one hand while steaming the next piece of wall with the other.

STRIPPING WITH WATER

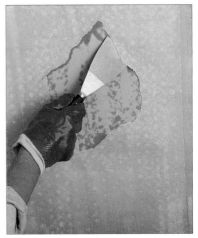

1 Measure hot water into a bucket and add the correct number of stripping tablets. Stir thoroughly until they are completely dissolved. Hot water alone can also be effective for soaking wallpaper.

2 Using a large brush, apply the solution to the paper, working from the top down. Do not soak more than a few square metres (yards) at a time or the paper will dry out before you have a chance to strip it off.

3 Allow the paper to soak for a few minutes, strip it away with a scraper. It is a good idea to clear up as you work, as otherwise the stripped paper will dry out on your dust sheets and become difficult to remove.

STRIPPING VINYL WALLPAPER

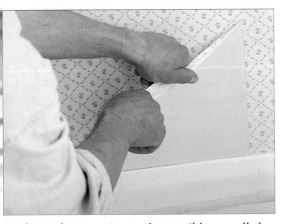

With vinyl papers, it may be possible to pull the top layer away from the backing paper, doing away with the need for a spiker/scorer. Never be tempted to leave the backing paper on the wall, however good its condition. It is rarely a sound surface on which to start decorating.

IDEAL TOOLS

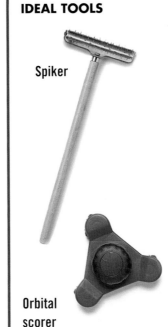

Spiker

Orbital scorer

With all types of wallpaper, it is a good idea to run a wallpaper spiker or orbital scorer over the paper prior to soaking. There are several different types of spiker/scorer on the market, but all work in the same way: they aim to perforate the top layer, allowing moisture underneath the paper to aid the stripping process.

Filling ceilings and walls

Cracks and holes in plasterwork are extremely common. They are caused either by slight movement in the building structure or just everyday wear and tear. To repair these defects, there are a number of different fillers available. Flexible fillers are best used in areas of potentially high movement, such as in cracks around door architraves. Pre-mixed and fine surface fillers come ready to use in a tub. However, powder filler is by far the most common type used. It is mixed up with water, as and when it is needed.

TOOLS: Filling knife, dusting brush, 25mm (1in) paintbrush, caulking blade, sanding block, hammer

MATERIALS: Powder filler, water, fine-grade sandpaper, newspaper, batten, nails

1 Use the edge of a clean filling knife or scraper to rake out and clean up the damaged area. Brush out any loose debris with a dusting brush.

2 Pour the amount of powder filler required on to a clean board. An old paint tub lid is ideal for this purpose. When estimating how much you should mix up at a time, bear in mind that the filler will remain workable for approximately one hour. Gradually add water, mixing the filler into a creamy yet firm consistency.

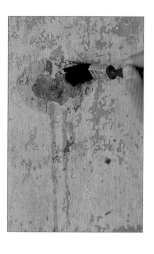

3 Dampen the hole and the area around it with water. This lengthens the drying time so the filler is less likely to shrink. It also helps the filler and the plaster to bond.

IDEAL TOOL

When faced with an old wall that has many small cracks, a caulking blade helps to cover a large surface area very quickly. Use it in the same manner as a filling knife. It is also excellent for wide holes as its large blade can rest on the edges of the hole, keeping the filler level.

4 Load some filler on to the filling knife and draw it across the hole, using the flexibility of the knife to firmly press the filler into the hole. You may need to draw the filling knife across the hole two or three times to ensure that the area has been covered completely and that the filler is firmly in place. Always try to fill the hole slightly 'proud' of the surrounding area, to allow for a small amount of shrinkage. When the hole is filled, use the filling knife to clean off any excess filler from the wall around the hole to avoid any extra sanding when the filler has dried.

5 Sand the area when dry with a fine grade of sandpaper. Then run your fingers over the hole to check that it feels smooth and flush with the rest of the wall. If it is not, dust it off, wet as before and use a thin skim of filler to make good any indentations. With particularly deep holes, trying to fill them with just one load of filler can be difficult. Bulging will occur where the filler is unable to bond with the surrounding area. In this case, it may be necessary to use several thin coats to gradually build up the filler until it is level with the surrounding wall.

FILLING DEEP CRACKS

Sometimes it is necessary to fill a large, deep crack, perhaps in the corner of a room. Prior to filling, screw up a length of newspaper and, using a filling knife, press it very firmly into the crack. This will give the filler a base to sit on while it dries.

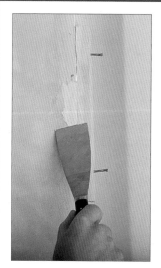

FILLING A CORNER

To repair an external corner, fix a length of wooden batten flush to one edge of the corner securing it in place with two nails. Fill the hole using a filling knife or caulking blade. When the filler has dried, sand the area, remove the batten and repeat the process on the adjacent corner edge. Finally, fill the four nail holes made by tacking on the batten. This technique will reproduce the original square corner edge.

Cleaning down and sealing

Before either lining or wallpaper is applied, cleaning down and sealing are essential processes. They stabilise the surfaces before decoration – of any type – is added. Painting or papering over unstable or dirty areas may look good at first, but the result will quickly deteriorate. Although these all-important initial steps cannot be seen when decorating is completed, they will add to the quality of the finish and make sure it lasts.

TOOLS: Bucket, sponge, 37 and 100mm (1½ and 4in) paintbrushes, gloves

MATERIALS: Damp sealant/ oil-based undercoat, aerosol stain block, size/ wallpaper paste, sugar soap, PVA adhesive, water

SEALING

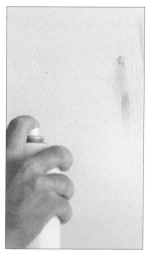

1 Damp stains are common, but can be cured with the correct treatment. Consult a professional if a damp patch is clearly active as you may have an exterior problem that needs attention. If the stain is old and dry, or the problem has been cured, apply a proprietary damp sealant or an oil-based undercoat over the area.

2 Some nondescript stains keep persisting despite using a sealant. Proprietary aerosol stain blocks will generally take care of marks that are the most difficult to cover.

3 If working on new plaster, first apply a coat of size or diluted wallpaper paste. Either of these will seal the surface to ensure good paper adhesion and uniform absorption, and will also allow you to manoeuvre the paper freely on the wall.

CLEANING

1 All ceilings and walls to be papered should be cleaned down using a solution of sugar soap or mild detergent. Mix the sugar soap powder with warm water according to the manufacturer's instructions on the packet.

2 Wear protective gloves when using a solution of sugar soap as it irritates the skin. Make sure you clean all surfaces thoroughly, removing any dust and impurities. When the surface is clean, rinse off the sugar soap using clean water and a sponge. Allow to dry completely before continuing to decorate.

4 PVA adhesive is ideal for sealing porous or dusty surfaces as it bonds the wall surface together and acts as a size before papering. Read the manufacturer's guidelines for mixing, but 1 part PVA to 5 parts water is the usual dilution used.

5 Apply the PVA solution liberally, making sure of good coverage. 'Pick up' and brush in any drips or runs that may occur. When dry, run your hand over the surface to check whether it is still dusty or powdery. If so, add a second coat.

PAPERING OVER GLOSS PAINT

On surfaces that have been painted previously with gloss paint, it is necessary to sand the painted surface to provide a key. This enables the paper to adhere to the wall.

SIZING EACH SURFACE

As well as sizing bare wall surfaces before hanging lining paper, remember to size lining paper before hanging the patterned wallpaper over it. This will make it much easier to manoeuvre the wallpaper into its correct position on the wall.

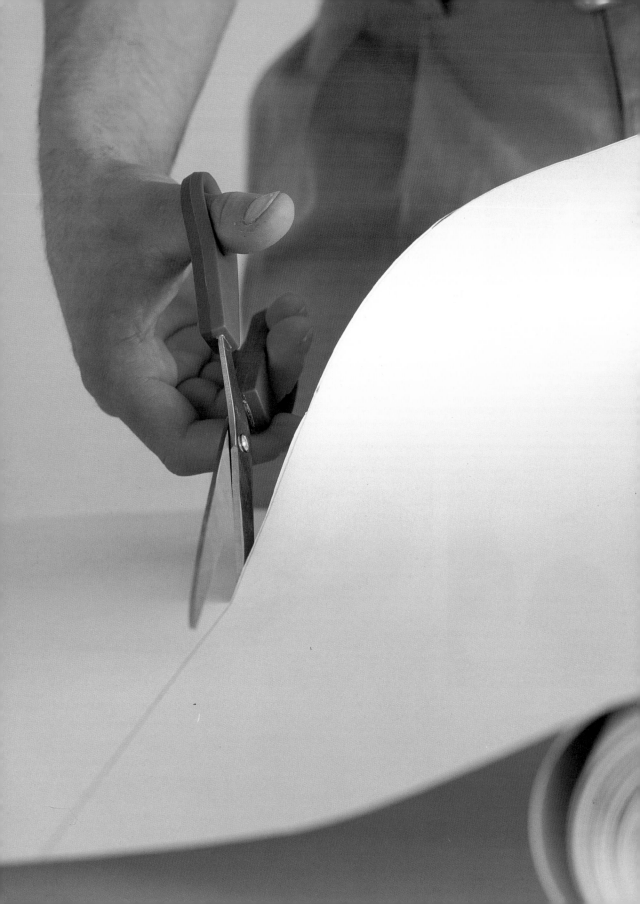

Lining

Whether you are eventually going to paint or wallpaper a room, using lining paper on walls and ceilings makes all the difference for a professional rather than an amateur finish. Lining paper smooths out imperfections and gives an ideal surface on which to decorate.

There is a commonly held belief that you must line horizontally before wallpapering, and vertically for painting purposes. The choice is a purely practical one, however: the aim is to cover the ceiling and/or walls with the fewest number of lengths, to make best use of time and effort.

This chapter will show you how to approach lining a room using the correct techniques, and how to overcome any problems that you may encounter.

This chapter contains

Preparation

Before starting to hang any lining paper, decide how many rolls are needed to complete the job. Using a tape measure and the table to the right, you can be surprisingly accurate.

The diagram on page 23 illustrates the best way to calculate surface areas. There is no right or wrong place to start, as each surface should be treated as separate to the next. Mentally divide your room into different areas (see below right) and decide on the most practical direction to line; this will help you decide your order of work. Begin with the ceiling as it is, in fact, easier than most walls because there are fewer obstacles to work around.

When lining a wall horizontally, start at the top and work down, as working from the bottom up may cause problems when joining the paper at higher levels, especially after papering around an obstacle such as a doorway, window or fireplace.

TOOLS: Tape measure, pocket calculator, pencil and paper, 2 buckets, measuring jug, stirring stick

MATERIALS: Packet of wallpaper paste, water

1 When setting out equipment it is important to be well organised. Place buckets of paste and clean water under the table to save space and to avoid accidents. Always keep your table clean and clear of obstacles. Try to keep everything to hand to save time and energy.

2 When mixing up paste ensure all the equipment is clean. Always read the manufacturer's instructions as they can vary between different brands of paste. Measure out the correct quantity of cold water using a measuring jug.

3 Start to stir the water, then sprinkle the powder slowly into the bucket. Continue to stir for 2 minutes after adding all the paste. Leave it to stand for another 3 minutes, then stir again to ensure there are no lumps. It is now ready to use.

USING A PLATFORM

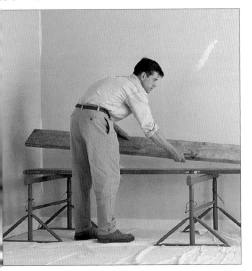

Working on a safe, solid platform is very important, especially when papering a ceiling. Trestles are excellent supports, but two step-ladders with a sturdy plank are a good compromise. Remember to have extra support underneath the middle of the plank when covering a large area.

MEASURING UP

Follow steps 1 and 2 on page 23, and calculate the amount of lining paper needed from the table below. There is no need to add on any extra for pattern repeat when using lining paper.

ROLLS OF LINING PAPER NEEDED

Total Surface Area to Line		No of rolls	
sq m	sq yd		
5	6	1	For every additional
10	12	2	5sq m (6sq yd), add
15	18	3	one roll of lining paper.

Standard roll of lining paper is 56cm x 10.05m = 5.628sq m (22in x 11yd = 6¾sq yd). The excess of 0.628sq m (¾sq yd) per roll allows for both trimming and wastage.

If you are not using standard rolls, simply work out the surface area of the rolls you are using and create your own table by the same method as above.

Order of work

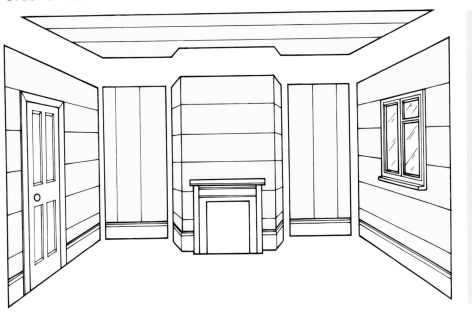

DOUBLE LINING

On particularly uneven walls, the final finish may look better if you apply two layers of lining paper before the top wallpaper. Ensure that the joins on the second layer do not coincide with the seams of the first.

Cutting and pasting

When cutting lengths of lining paper always add 10cm (4in) to your basic measurement to allow a 5cm (2in) overlap at each end for final trimming.

After pasting, leave the paper for about 5 minutes for the paste to soak into the paper. This makes it less likely to bubble, more pliable and easier to work with. Once you start work it is advisable to write a number on each length: you may have up to three or four lengths soaking at any one time, and this will keep them in the correct order.

TOOLS: Pasting table, tape measure, pencil, steel rule, scissors, pasting brush, paper-hanging brush, sponge

MATERIALS: Lining paper, bucket of wallpaper paste, water

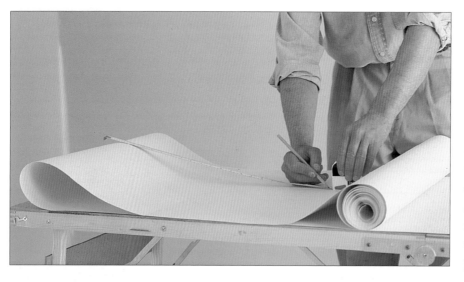

1 Carefully unroll the lining paper along the length of the pasting table. If long pieces of paper are going to be needed, gently fold the paper back on itself along the table. Use a tape measure to work out the length of paper required. Make a pencil mark in the centre of the paper where the first piece is to be cut.

2 Keep the edges of the length of paper flush with the edges of the table. This will help to ensure a square cut. Place a straight edge at the pencil mark, check it is square and draw a line along its length.

3 Cut a neat, straight line along the pencil line. Then lie the paper flat along the table with the excess paper falling over one end. Use the paper-hanging brush to hold the other end of the paper still.

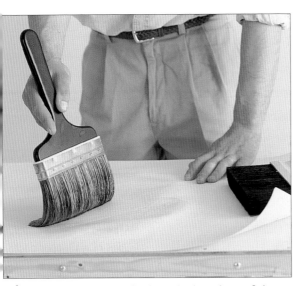

4 Line up the paper flush with the edges of the table, to avoid getting paste on the face of the paper. Apply the paste evenly, working from the centre outwards, ensuring the whole area is covered.

5 Once the paper on the table is pasted, gently fold the pasted end over, starting a concertina. Pull this along to one end of the table, again with the paper-hanging brush anchoring the other end.

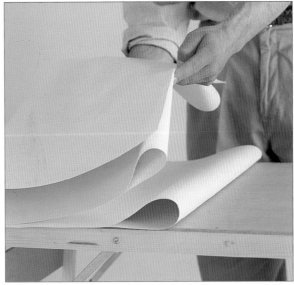

6 Continue to paste the remaining paper, working up to the end of the table. Always make sure that the paste is applied evenly, and that all areas of the paper are covered with paste. Try to avoid getting any paste on the other (unpasted) side of the paper.

7 Keep folding the paper back on itself to make up a finished concertina. When all the paper has been pasted, remove it from the table and leave it to soak for the required time. Wipe the table down with a slightly damp sponge to clean up any excess paste.

Ceilings

Always try to line across the longest dimension of the room as fewer lengths will be required, and this will save time.

Make sure that you have a solid platform from which to work. Trestles and planks are ideal as they enable you to get close to the wall–ceiling junction at both ends of the platform. Adjust its height so that the top of your head is 25–30cm (9–12in) from the ceiling.

Lining the ceiling is not as difficult as it may appear. Once the first length is hung and a straight edge established, subsequent lengths become easier and less time consuming.

TOOLS: Trestles and plank, paper-hanging brush, pencil, scissors, small brush for pasting edges, sponge

MATERIALS: Lining paper, bucket of wallpaper paste, water

1 Arrange the trestles and plank under the area where you wish to start. Carefully lay out the concertina along the plank. Pick up one end of the paper.

2 Start papering at the edge of the ceiling. Take care to keep the paper edge parallel with the length of the adjacent wall. Using the paper-hanging brush push the paper into the junction, allowing for 5cm (2in) overlap.

3 When the paper is held securely at one end, move slowly along the plank, brushing the paper from the centre out in a herringbone fashion. Keep the edge of the paper tight to the wall using it as a guide. Brush the length into position and repeat step 2 at the opposite end.

4 When the length is hung, run a pencil along where the wall and ceiling meet to make a straight line. Alternatively, run a pair of scissors along to make a crease.

EASIER CEILINGS
Papering a ceiling is easier and less tiring with two people. One can hold the paper while the other manoeuvres it into place.

5 Carefully peel back the paper. Using the paper-hanging scissors, cut a neat, straight edge along the pencil guideline or scissor crease.

6 Push the paper back into position. Work along the length, checking for bubbles or lifting at the edge. Apply extra paste to edges where needed.

7 After each length is hung, immediately wipe off any surplus paste from all the surfaces, or it will stain them.

Hang the next length in the same way as the first but place the edge of the new length adjacent to that of the first. Slide the paper into position making a neat butt join.

Walk down the plank brushing out the paper, making sure you keep the two edges of the join completely flush. Trim off at each end as before.

DEALING WITH GAPS
If the wall is not square, you will find that a gap appears along the wall–ceiling junction as you work along the length of the ceiling. A small gap of 5mm or less can be filled (see page 43), but if a larger gap appears, simply move the paper closer to the wall, allowing an overlap on to the wall. This overlap can be trimmed using the technique shown in steps 4–6 above.

Ceiling roses

Most ceilings have at least one light fitting and by far the most common is the ceiling rose. Two methods can be used to paper around them. The first, shown in steps 1–5, is to pull the pendant through a cut in the paper. The second and more reliable method, shown in the box on page 39, is to measure the distance between the starting wall and the ceiling rose to ensure that a seam between lengths will coincide with the pendant.

TOOLS: Trestles and plank, paper-hanging brush, scissors, craft knife, small brush for pasting edges, sponge, screwdriver

MATERIALS: Lining paper, bucket of wallpaper paste, water, clean cloth

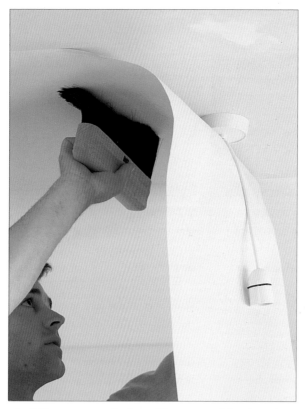

ELECTRICAL SAFETY
Always remember to turn off the power supply before undertaking any work around electrical fittings.

1 When you reach the ceiling rose with a length of pasted paper, gently brush the paper over the pendant, so that you can see where the rose is located in relation to the paper.

2 Support the unfixed side of the paper with one hand. Using scissors, carefully mark the location of the centre of the rose on the underside of the paper. Make a small cut.

3 Gently pull the pendant through the cut, taking care not to tear the paper. Then brush the remaining length of paper away, continuing on to the wall on the other side of the room.

4 Using the scissors, make a series of small cuts out to the edge of the rose. Work right round the rose, but do not cut any further than the edge of the plastic circle itself.

5 Crease around the edge of the rose and trim with a craft knife. Brush out any remaining bubbles from the entire length, and wipe off any excess paste from the pendant with a dry cloth.

METHOD 2: SEAM JOIN

1 Turn off the power supply. Unscrew the rose's casing by hand and loosen off the retaining screws. Then allow the entire pendant to drop approximately 5cm (2in).

2 Using the paper-hanging brush, tuck in the paper edges underneath the rose. Tighten the screws and screw the ceiling rose casing back into position.

Walls

Lining paper on walls can be hung either horizontally or vertically. The choice is purely a practical one. Vertical lining is ideal for small alcoves as fewer lengths are required, whereas a long wall can be quickly covered with horizontal lengths. Vertical lining uses a vertical corner of the wall as a straight edge, whereas horizontal lining takes its guide from where the wall and the ceiling meet.

As horizontal lengths are normally longer than vertical lengths, a much larger concertina is required. To overcome this problem, make the folds smaller so that the concertina is more compact and easier to manage with one hand.

TOOLS: Trestles and plank, paper-hanging brush, pencil, scissors, craft knife, small brush for pasting edges, sponge

MATERIALS: Lining paper, bucket of wallpaper paste, water

HORIZONTAL LINING

1 Start papering at the top of the wall leaving a 5cm (2in) overlap around the corner on to the next area of wall. Line up the top edge of the paper with the wall and ceiling junction. If the wall–ceiling junction is not square, move the paper to overlap onto the ceiling and trim as usual when the remainder of the length is hung.

2 Slowly release the folds of the concertina, smoothing the paper along the wall using a paper-hanging brush. Brushing from the centre of the paper outwards, continue along to the other corner, keeping the top edge of the paper flush with the wall–ceiling junction.

3 Mark a line at the corner with a pencil, or crease the corner with scissors, then gently pull the paper away from the wall. Trim with the scissors or a craft knife.

4 Push the paper back into the corner with the brush. Extra paste may be needed if the edge of the paper has dried out during trimming. Repeat steps 3 and 4 at the other end of the length.

CROOKED ROOMS

If the wall or ceiling is very crooked (and it has been necessary to overlap paper on to the ceiling) you will be unable to use the wall–ceiling junction as a guideline to hang the entire length. So that you do not find yourself papering this first length at a sharp angle, it is wise to hold a spirit level at the bottom edge to ensure that the first length is hung straight. When lining vertically, a spirit level can also be used as a guideline when unsquare walls are causing problems.

VERTICAL LINING

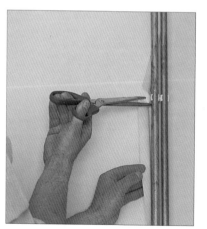

1 Vertical lining is an excellent way to deal with problem areas such as pipes. Start the first length flush with the pipes and push the paper behind them so the join will be hidden.

2 Mark the location of the pipe clips with a pencil and make two small cuts to the edge of the clips. Push the paper around the clips and trim off the excess paper.

3 Cut another length and butt-join it to the previously hung paper. Smooth and trim as before. Wipe any excess paste off the pipes as it will otherwise react with paint, if used.

Corners

When lining, the only corners you need to paper around are external (that is, those that stick out). At internal corners it is better to begin or end paper, because trying to bend it around the corner usually causes bubbles and problems with adhesion. Using filler on internal corners, as shown here, is a far wiser and ultimately neater option. If you have difficulty with an external corner that is uneven or not square, a manufactured butt join is the ideal solution.

TOOLS: Trestles and plank, paper-hanging brush, scissors, steel rule, craft knife, sponge

MATERIALS: Lining paper, bucket of wallpaper paste, water, flexible filler, powder filler, sandpaper, cloth

EXTERNAL CORNERS

1 Approach the external corner holding the horizontal concertina in one hand. Use the other hand to push the paper up to the corner edge, keeping the horizontal edge of the length of paper flush with the edge of the ceiling or the paper above, forming a neat butt join.

2 Fold the paper around the corner using the paper-hanging brush to expel any bubbles. Make sure that the top edge of the paper is not overlapping the paper already hung above it.

3 Run your fingers gently down the corner to check for any wrinkles or creases. Smooth them out, if necessary. Once the corner is neat and problem-free, proceed along the wall with the rest of the length.

UNEVEN EXTERNAL CORNERS

1 For an uneven corner, bend the horizontal length around the corner and trim off all except a 5cm (2in) overlap. Do this with each (horizontal) length on the corner. Hang the next length (on the next section of wall) vertically, on top of the overlaps.

2 On the wall with the vertical length, place a straight edge 3cm (1¼in) from the corner. Using a craft knife, cut a straight line down the straight edge. Then move the straight edge and repeat the process, so continuing the cut from ceiling to skirting.

3 Pull back the paper and gently remove the excess (overlapping) strips of paper. Push the paper back into position using the paper-hanging brush. Finally, wipe the area with a damp sponge to remove any excess paste.

INTERNAL CORNERS

1 Because we recommend trimming all lengths at an internal corner, for a perfect finish, run a bead of flexible filler along all internal corners, and along the skirting board top.

2 Smooth along the filler with a wetted finger. This will neaten the finish, and prevent the edges of the paper from lifting later. Wipe off any excess filler with a clean damp cloth.

FILLING GAPS

Small gaps between lengths are sometimes unavoidable. These can be overcome using a fine surface filler, and then sanded smooth.

Doors and obstacles

Some room features – such as door surrounds, flush windows and fireplaces – protrude out from the wall, and lining paper must be cut to fit around them. No matter what the obstacle, the technique used is much the same. A neat and exact finish is produced by precisely trimming into angles and along edges. The examples shown here include a fireplace that needs complex trimming, and a door because, quite simply, every room has one.

TOOLS: Trestles and plank, paper-hanging brush, pencil, scissors, craft knife, small brush for pasting edges, sponge

MATERIALS: Lining paper, bucket of wallpaper paste, water

FIREPLACES

1 When the paper reaches the fireplace, allow it to flap over the top corner of the mantlepiece. Make a cut diagonally towards the upper part of the corner, taking care that the paper below the cut does not tear under its own weight.

2 Having made this initial cut, ignore the paper fold on top of the fireplace for the time being. With the aid of the paper-hanging brush and scissors, push the paper gently into the angles of the mantlepiece making small right-angled cuts to allow it to lie flat on the wall.

3 Trim the small flaps with a craft knife, taking care to get as close as possible to the moulding, and without leaving any gaps. Continue to paper along the top of the mantlepiece and repeat steps 1–3 at the other corner. Then trim the fold on top of the mantlepiece.

4 It is vital to clean the excess paste off ornate obstacles immediately in order to prevent later staining or discolouration. Use a clean dampened sponge, and pay particular attention to paste that may have found its way into intricate details.

DOORS

2 Both hands now freed, feel for the corner of the architrave. Cut diagonally towards this point with scissors. Carefully draw back the excess paper hanging over the door. Using the paper-hanging brush, firmly push the paper covering the wall above the door into the edge of the architrave. Do the same with the other corner of the architrave.

3 Using a craft knife, trim away the excess paper, working carefully around the side and top edges of the door architrave.

1 Allow the length of paper to fall over the corner of the door architrave. Continue to hang the length along the rest of the wall, loosely attaching it to the wall surface.

Recessed windows

The technique for lining around a recessed window combines a number of steps already covered in this chapter. However, the order in which you hang the various lengths of paper is vital to produce the best possible finish. The particular method shown here will also come in useful when tackling similar types of shapes and obstacles, such as recessed doors or alcoves.

TOOLS: Trestles and plank, paper-hanging brush, scissors, craft knife, small brush for pasting edges, steel rule, sponge

MATERIALS: Lining paper, wallpaper paste, water

1 Hang the first length of paper horizontally, as usual, allowing the paper to span right across the recess. When you have made sure the paper is correctly butt-joined to the previous length, return to the window and make two vertical cuts approximately 1.5cm (⅝in) in from the corners of the recess. Carefully continue these cuts right up to the top edge of the window recess.

2 Starting in the middle, use the paper-hanging brush to push the flap of paper you have made back into the recess, expelling any air bubbles as you do so. Move the brush along the edge continuing the process until the paper is properly in place on the ceiling of the recess.

3 Make sure the paper has been firmly positioned in the junction between the window frame and the upper part of the recess, before trimming as usual.

4 Fold the 1.5cm (⅝in) flap around the corner of the vertical recess using your brush and fingers to expel any air bubbles if necessary. Add extra paste to the edge of the paper if it has dried out too quickly. Hang the next length, again allowing a flap of paper approximately 1.5cm (⅝in) wide to fold around into the recess. Repeat this process at the opposite side of the window recess.

5 Depending on the height of the window recess, you may need to hang further lengths of paper before finally reaching the window sill. At the sill, carefully trim the paper using a series of right-angled cuts, moulding the paper around the corner of the sill and underneath it. Once you have successfully dealt with one side, repeat this process when the paper reaches the opposite corner of the sill.

6 Measure and cut a panel of paper to finish off each vertical return of the recess. Line up the straight edge of the paper with the vertical corner, covering the trimmed overlaps of the previous lengths.

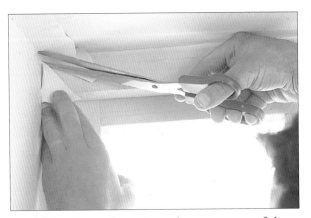

7 Make diagonal cuts into the top corner of the recess. Repeat this at the bottom corner, to assist final trimming. Any small gaps can be filled using the methods shown on page 43.

REFINING TECHNIQUE
You may find that this technique of overlapping different pieces of lining paper does not produce a completely flat surface, as the small cuts around the vertical, external corners of the recess may form an impression in the paper pasted over the top. Faced with this problem, there are two points to consider. First, it is likely that curtains will eventually cover these imperfections. Second, as you become more skilled, you may prefer to try the manufactured butt-join technique shown in Uneven External Corners (see page 43).

Electrical wall fittings

It goes without saying that light switches and electrical sockets are very common features on walls. It often appears to be difficult to paper around them neatly but if care is taken, they need not present a problem. It is important to make a neat job of light switches as every time you enter or leave a room, your eyes are naturally drawn towards them. Whatever their size or shape, the technique for coping with them remains the same.

Always remember to turn off the electricity at the mains or consumer unit before working near any electrical fitting.

TOOLS: Paper-hanging brush, pencil, scissors, screwdriver, craft knife, small brush for pasting edges, sponge

MATERIALS: Lining paper, bucket of wallpaper paste, water, dry cloth

1 Turn off the electricity at the mains. Paper directly over the top of the power point or switch, butt-joining the paper, as usual.

2 Brush gently over the fixture, allowing it to form an impression in the paper. Take care not to tear the paper when carrying out this step.

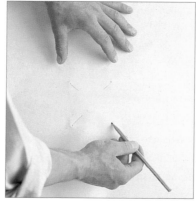

3 Holding the paper firmly over the switch or power point, make a small diagonal pencil mark, 5mm (¼in) in from each of its corners.

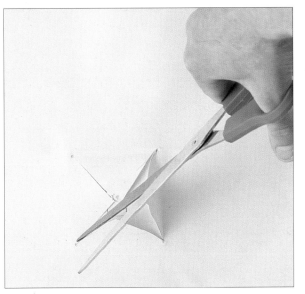

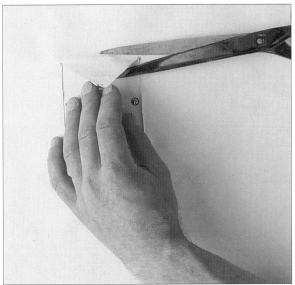

4 Using scissors, carefully make four diagonal cuts from the centre of the switch out to the pencil marks.

5 Trim off each of the four flaps, just inside the outer edge of the switch, so that a small amount of overlap remains over the switch plate.

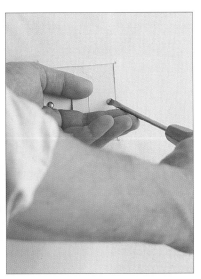

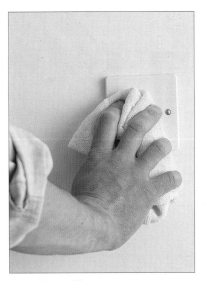

6 Unscrew the two retaining screws that hold the face plate on to the switch itself. It is not necessary to unscrew them completely, but just far enough to move the face plate a little way out from the wall.

7 Ease the face plate out from the wall, rotating it slightly from side to side. Be careful when pushing the face plate through the paper as erratic movements will tear it. Use the brush to push the paper behind the plate.

8 Wipe off any excess paste with a dry cloth. Put the face plate back and tighten up the screws, making sure the small paper flaps are firmly tucked behind the face plate. Take care not to over-tighten the screws.

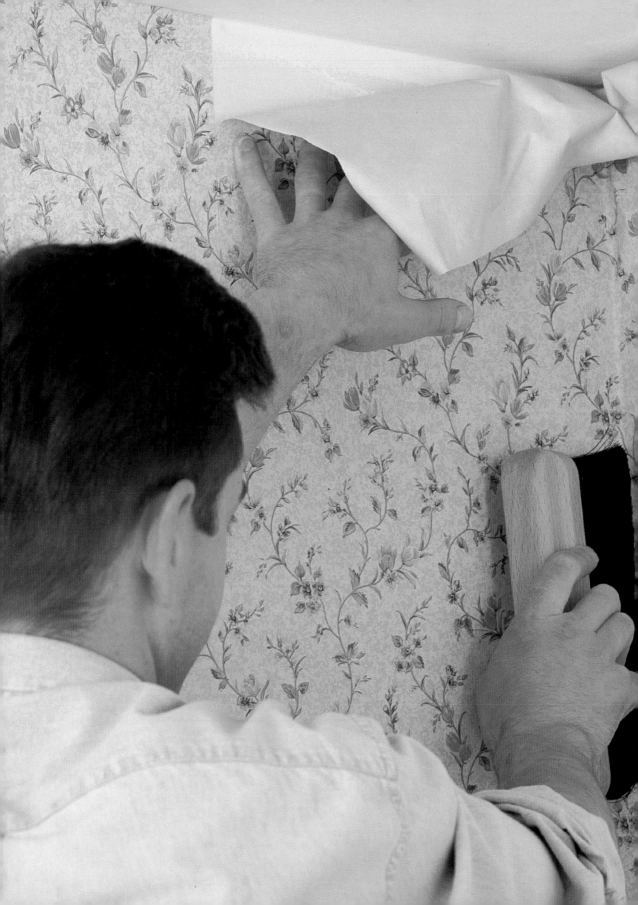

Wallpapering

Hanging the wallpaper itself can be the most enjoyable part of paper hanging. Although there is a huge variety of papers, the vast majority are hung in the same way. This chapter explains the whole process, from where to start to papering around difficult obstacles.

Always read the wallpaper manufacturer's guidelines to check whether there are any specific requirements or instructions for your paper.

Where to start

Deciding where to start papering depends on the shape and the layout of the room, and on the wallpaper design. Look at whether there is a main focal point, such as a chimney breast. If so, and if you are using a large pattern, it should be centralised. With smaller or free-match patterns this is not an issue, so it is best to start close to a corner on a plain wall that does not have any obstacles.

TOOLS: Step-ladder, tape measure, pencil, spirit level, hammer, nail, plumb line

MATERIALS: Wallpaper

CHECKING THE PAPER

Make sure that the batch number on each roll is the same as all the others. Unwrap one of the rolls and check for any pattern imperfections or shading differences in the paper. If you do find any problems they are likely to be present in the rest of the batch. Manufacturers will generally not accept liability if more than one roll is opened, so this initial check is vital.

CENTRALISATION

Correct centralisation of wallpaper creates a well-balanced effect. The way to achieve this requires some thought, as some papers have the central pattern joining on a seam, whereas on others the central pattern will be in the middle of the length or even slightly offset.

The best method to get the pattern centred is to hold a 'dry' cut length in what will be its approximate central position above the mantlepiece, to make a pencil mark at its side and to draw a vertical guideline with the spirit level. When you come to apply this first length, use the guideline to position the paper. Then use a tape measure and spirit level to make any final adjustments to make sure the main pattern is right in the middle of the chimney breast.

Having positioned the first length, the rest of the chimney breast should be completed before the rest of the room.

▲ Poor centralisation can lead to a totally unbalanced effect.

▲ The balanced effect of good centralisation.

WHERE TO START

CENTRALISATION REQUIRED

1 First length
2 Finish chimney breast
3 Complete room

NO CENTRALISATION REQUIRED

1 First length
2 Continue around room
3 Final length to join in corner

USING A PLUMB LINE

A plumb line can give a reliable vertical guideline. Hammer a small nail into the wall close to the ceiling, and hang the plumb line. Make a series of pencil marks along the length of the string, and join them up with a steel rule.

NO CENTRALISATION REQUIRED

1 If pattern centralising is not required, start near an internal corner. Measure 2cm (1in) less than your wallpaper's width away from the corner, and make a mark with a pencil.

2 Place a long spirit level vertically against this mark and draw a pencil line down its complete length. This acts as a guide for your first length which should be hung on the opposite side of the line to the corner – not going into the corner itself. To the other side of the line, an overlap has been allowed for (ie, the 2cm (1in)). This will be used when you have papered all the way around the room and need to make a join in the corner (see diagram above).

Measuring and cutting

Careful and precise measuring avoids expensive mistakes (if the paper is cut too short) and unnecessary wastage (if it is cut too long). The task is made easier if you are using a free-match paper, such as vertical stripes, as no pattern matching is necessary. However, much more care is needed when dealing with patterned wallpapers, especially those with a large repeat.

TOOLS: Pasting table, tape measure, pencil, steel rule, scissors

MATERIALS: Wallpaper

MEASURING SMALL REPEATS

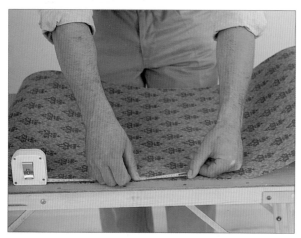

With small repeat patterns – for example of 5–10cm (2–4in) – it is best to add on to the wall height 10cm (4in) (that is, two times 5cm or 2in). This extra allows enough for trimming at each end, plus the length of the repeat. By working in this way you can cut a number of standard lengths at the start of the job, saving time by reducing the stop–start process of measuring, cutting and pasting for every length.

If you do cut a number of lengths at the beginning of the job, be sure to check first that the ceiling height is reasonably consistent all the way around the room.

MEASURING LARGE REPEATS

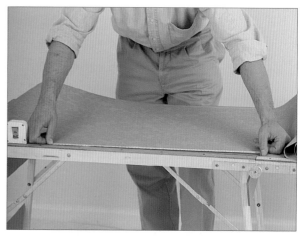

An option for larger patterns is to match the next length 'dry' to the previous length, and cut the right size, leaving enough excess just for trimming. This may be more laborious but will lead to less wastage, especially for offset patterns. Always use this technique for cutting lengths for small areas.

MEASURING PATTERN REPEAT
Most manufacturers state the size of the pattern repeat on the roll label. Whether this is the case or not, it is always best to check the size for yourself and take a precise measurement.

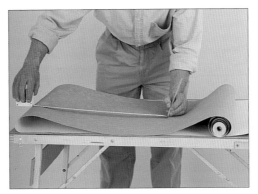

2 Unroll the paper along the pasting table. It is usually necessary to fold the paper back on itself for measuring, as most lengths will be longer than the table. Make a small mark with a pencil at the required length.

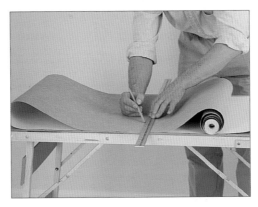

3 Always make an effort to keep the edge of the paper flush with the long edge of the table to ensure a square cut. Place a straight edge against the pencil mark and draw a line along its length, across the paper.

1 Measure the exact height of the wall from the ceiling to the top of the skirting board.

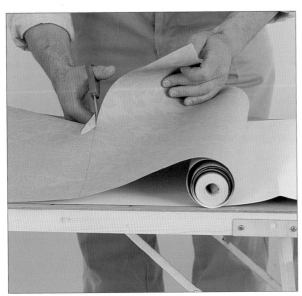

4 Use scissors to make a neat straight cut along the pencil line. It needn't be exactly even as the end of the paper will be trimmed eventually.

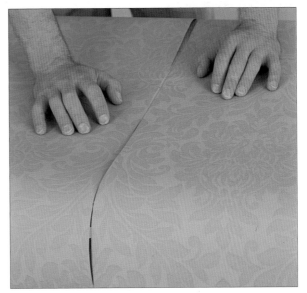

5 Prior to hanging the first length, it is worth having a 'dry run' to match the pattern as some are more subtle and less defined than others.

Pasting up

Most wallpaper is stuck to the wall by one of three methods. Ready-pasted paper is soaked in water to activate the paste, and some papers are hung 'dry' with the paste applied to the wall. However, the most common type uses special wallpaper paste that is brushed on to the paper before hanging. The pasting itself is simple, but it is important to keep the length of paper organised and tidy to avoid damaging it and getting unwanted paste on other surfaces.

TOOLS: Pasting table, 2 buckets, stirring stick, sponge, measuring jug, pasting brush, paper-hanging brush, scissors

MATERIALS: Wallpaper, paste, water

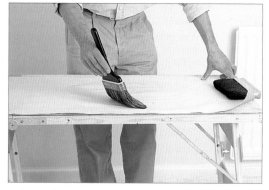

1 To mix the paste, make sure that all the equipment is clean. Measure out the correct amount of cold water into the bucket, following the paste-manufacturer's guidelines. Slowly sprinkle the paste into the water, stirring vigorously to ensure even dispersal. Most pastes should be stirred thoroughly, for 2–3 minutes, after the whole sachet has been added. Let the paste stand for a further 2–3 minutes, give it another quick stir and it is ready to use.

2 Unroll the measured length of paper, and weigh it down to stop it rolling back up; a paper-hanging brush is ideal for this. Be sure to line up the edge of the paper with the table edge to reduce the possibility of getting paste on the patterned side of the paper. Some wallpapers may stain if paste is allowed to dry on its patterned side, so remove excess paste immediately with a damp sponge. Apply the paste evenly, brushing from the centre outwards, covering the whole surface of the paper with a thin film of paste.

USING THE CORRECT PASTE
Always check the precise paste recommendations supplied with the wallpaper and follow specific instructions about the type of paste to use, as the chemical make-up of some pastes may be suitable only for some papers. Paste tends to be available in two forms: ready-mixed or powdered. Although ready-mixed paste is convenient, it is more economical – and quite easy – to mix your own.

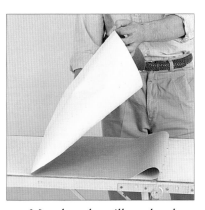

3 Most lengths will tend to be longer than the table. Once the area of paper covering the table has been pasted, gently fold the pasted end over on itself, starting a concertina.

4 Move the concertina of folded, pasted paper back along the table so that it rests squarely right at one end. Again, use a weight to hold down the unpasted end of the paper. Continue to paste the remainder of the length.

SOAKING TIME

All pasted wallpaper must have a soaking time of up to 15 minutes; always check the paper-manufacturer's guidelines for the exact length of time. Soaking allows the paper to expand and become more pliable. It will then be less likely to bubble as it dries.

5 With the entire length of paper now pasted, continue to fold it into the concertina. Do your best to support the paper as it is folded and take great care that it does not crease, as creases will be visible once it is hung.

6 Carefully pick up the completed concertina and put it to one side for the required soaking time. On the reverse side of the paper, write the time the paper will be ready to be applied to the wall. This will ensure that all the lengths get exactly the same soaking time, and will help to keep them in the right order if you have more than one length pasted and soaking at a time.

7 In between pasting each length, do not forget to wipe the pasting table down with a clean, damp sponge. This will ensure that leftover paste does not get on to the patterned side of the next length laid on the table.

Ready-pasted and paste-the-wall papers

Ready-pasted paper is becoming more common, mainly because it is easy to use. When the paper is made, dry paste is added to the rear side. This is reactivated with water by soaking the paper in a trough before it is stuck to the wall.

Many manufacturers suggest that a trough should be placed at the bottom of the wall and the paper should be drawn out of it and applied directly to the wall. However, this may cause problems and the methods here are the most successful with all types of ready-pasted paper.

Other wall coverings are designed to be hung by adding paste to the wall rather than to the paper. These are called 'paste-the wall' papers.

TOOLS: Pasting table, wallpaper trough, bucket, sponge, pasting brush or roller, paper-hanging brush

MATERIALS: Wallpaper, paste, water

PASTE-THE-WALL PAPER

1 Using a pasting brush or a painting roller, thoroughly coat the wall with the appropriate paste on an area slightly wider than the paper.

2 Once the paste is spread evenly, hang the paper directly from the roll, or first cut it to length (see pages 54–55).

READY-PASTED PAPER

2 Fill the trough two-thirds full with cold water and position it at one end of the pasting table. Fully immerse the roll of paper in the trough and hold it under the water for the manufacturer's recommended soaking time. Agitate the roll slightly during soaking to expel any air bubbles, and to ensure that all the paper is coming into contact with the water.

1 Measure and cut the paper in the usual way (see pages 54–55). On the pasting table, loosely roll up the cut length, against its natural curl from the roll, so that the reverse, pre-pasted side is outermost.

3 Carefully pull the length out of the water, gradually drawing it on to the pasting table, patterned side down. Allow excess water to drain back into the trough. If the paper needs further soaking time, carry out steps 4 and 5. If the paper requires no further soaking time, fold up the bottom end of the paper (pasted sides together) to make it more manageable when carrying and applying it to the wall.

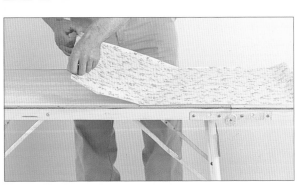

4 If extra soaking time is required, fold the top half of the paper back on itself as far as the central point of the length, pasted sides together, keeping the paper edges flush.

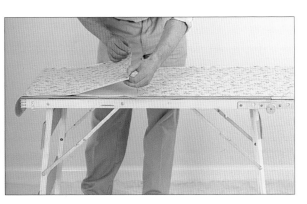

5 Fold the bottom half to the centre. This ensures even paste coverage and keeps the paper moist until it is ready to hang. Use a damp sponge to clean down the table between soaking the lengths.

EXTRA PASTE

Although ready-pasted paper does not use traditional wallpaper paste, it is sometimes useful to have a small amount handy as the edges may dry out. When hanging a length that requires intricate cutting and therefore considerable time (such as round an ornate mantlepiece or an archway), extra paste may then be added where necessary to ensure the edges are firmly stuck down.

Hanging the first length

Before hanging the first length of paper check which way it should be hung. With some patterns the direction may at first appear not to matter; however when on the wall the direction of some patterns can be critical. Manufacturers of free-match patterns often recommend that alternate lengths should be reversed to even out any minor differences in shading, so always read the label on the paper.

It is essential to take time when hanging the first length, not only to ensure it is level but also to make certain the balance of pattern is correct, especially with large designs (see pages 52–53).

TOOLS: Pasting table, 2 buckets, sponge, pasting brush, paper-hanging brush, wallpaper trough (if needed), step-ladder, scissors

MATERIALS: Wallpaper, paste, water

1 Place the first length on the wall, next to your pencil guideline (see pages 52–53). The top of the length should be at the wall–ceiling junction with a 5cm (2in) overlap on the ceiling, for trimming. Take care, especially when unfolding concertinas, that the paper does not tear.

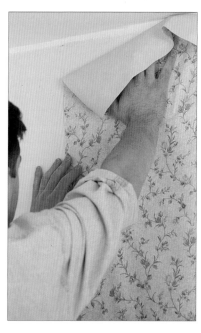

2 Now that the top section of the length of wallpaper is loosely attached to the wall at the correct height, slide the vertical edge of the paper into its final position next to the vertical pencil guideline.

3 Using the paper-hanging brush, firmly push the top edge of the paper into the wall–ceiling junction. Make sure the length of paper does not move from its correct vertical alignment in the process.

4 Move down the length of paper, brushing out any air bubbles or creases, working from the centre of the length outwards. Keep checking to make sure that the vertical edge of the paper is still aligned with the guideline.

5 With the top half of the paper hung securely in its final position, leave the bottom section untouched for the moment and return your attention to the wall–ceiling junction.

6 Run the blunt edge of the scissors along the paper crease in the wall–ceiling junction to give a guideline for trimming. Alternatively, a pencil may be used instead.

7 Pull the paper away from the wall and trim with scissors along the creased guideline. If the ceiling is slightly uneven it is often best to trim just above the line as this gives a better finish.

8 With the paper-hanging brush, push the trimmed edge firmly back into position at the wall–ceiling junction. Add a little extra paste if the edge has dried out during trimming.

Finishing the first length

With the top half of the first length of wallpaper in position and trimmed at the top (see pages 60–61), attention can now be given to the bottom section of the wallpaper that has not been attached to the wall.

At the bottom of a wall, uneven wall–skirting-board junctions can often be a problem. To deal with them use a similar technique to that for trimming at uneven ceilings: trim slightly below the creased guideline to compensate for the undulations in the wall, and thereby produce a neater trimmed edge.

TOOLS: Pasting table, 2 buckets, sponge, pasting brush, paper-hanging brush, wallpaper trough (if needed), scissors, step-ladder, craft knife, rotary trimmer

MATERIALS: Wallpaper, paste, water

1 Once the top half of the paper is securely in place and the top edge trimmed to fit, ease the bottom half of the paper away from the wall, releasing folds if necessary.

2 Using the paper-hanging brush, continue to work downwards, again expelling air bubbles and smoothing out the paper. Firmly push the paper into the wall–skirting junction.

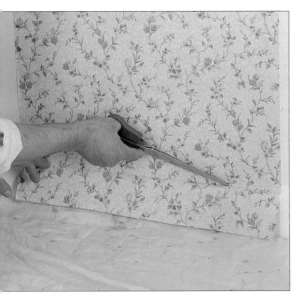
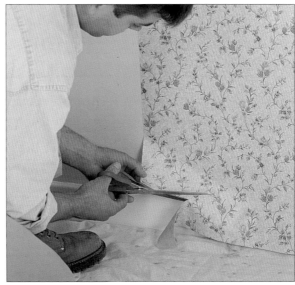

3 As with the top edge, use the scissors or a pencil to crease an exact trimming line along the junction between the wall and the skirting board. (See step 6, page 61.)

4 Pull the paper back and trim along the creased guideline. Once it is trimmed, push the edge back into the wall–skirting junction using the paper-hanging brush.

5 Finally, use a clean damp sponge to wipe off any excess paste from the ceiling, skirting board and wallpaper surface.

IDEAL TOOLS

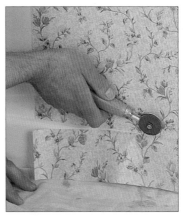

Craft knife
May be used for trimming instead of scissors. If possible, cut away from the body for obvious safety reasons. Change the blade at regular intervals to ensure a clean cut.

Rotary trimmer
Also useful for cutting paper, by running the circular blade along the guide crease. Use a dry cloth to keep the blade clean and free from paste build-up.

Pattern matching

When correctly butt-joined, most wallpaper patterns match together extremely well from one length to the next and you are rarely able to see the join.

Pattern matching can be divided broadly into three categories. Free match is where there is no specific point or design where lengths join; straight match is where there is a precise point to join lengths; and offset match is where the pattern is staggered between lengths but a precise point of join is still required. To match a precise pattern use the techniques laid out below.

TOOLS: Pasting table, 2 buckets, sponge, pasting brush, paper-hanging brush, wallpaper trough (if needed), step-ladder, scissors, craft knife, seam roller, spirit level

MATERIALS: Wallpaper, paste, water

1 Paste up the new length and place it on the wall as near to the pattern match as possible.

2 With the paper now loosely attached to the wall, slide the top half of the length flush with the edge of the previous length forming a tight butt join. At the same time, make any minor adjustments vertically to get a perfect pattern match.

3 Brush out the paper as usual, paying particular attention to the vertical edge to make sure that a neat butt join is continuing down the length of the paper and that the paper's pattern match is consistent all the way from ceiling to floor.

AVOIDING DRY EDGES

Wallpaper edges may dry out due to insufficient pasting or when tackling an awkward, time-consuming area. Keep your pasting brush handy to reapply paste where necessary.

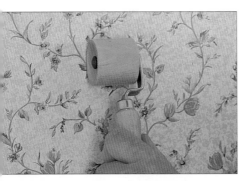

4 A seam roller may be used to gently run down the butt join to ensure good adhesion and a perfect flat finish. Do not use a seam roller with embossed papers as you may flatten the relief.

DEALING WITH PATTERN DROP

Problems with pattern-matching may occur when hanging some wallpapers, especially if hand-printed. Due to the way these papers are manufactured, some may have differences in pattern size or consistency throughout their length. By the time the paper reaches the lower part of the wall the pattern may have 'dropped'. If so, match the pattern at eye level rather than at the top, so that the area of paper that is seen most often has the best pattern match.

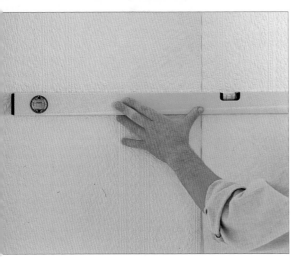

5 Some papers are difficult to get precisely level. On some straight-match papers the actual join may be a free match. For example, the paper may have a floral pattern in its centre, but the paper edges join on a vertical stripe design. If necessary, use a spirit level to check the horizontal line-up.

6 Free-match patterns, such as vertical stripes, are clearly the easiest to join as there is no particular match needed. However, make sure the butt join is precise, as free-match patterns will tend to show up poor joins whereas a busier floral design would disguise them.

Internal corners

All rooms have internal corners, so knowing the most successful technique to deal with them is essential. Trying to fold the wallpaper around an internal corner often causes problems with poor adhesion along the entire height of the corner crease. Furthermore, the wallpaper may be thrown off level because the corner is not totally square. Getting the paper to turn smoothly from one wall to the next is best achieved by dividing the wallpaper into two vertical strips during application.

TOOLS: Pasting table, 2 buckets, sponge, pasting brush, paper-hanging brush, wallpaper trough (if needed), step-ladder, tape measure, scissors, craft knife, spirit level, fitch

MATERIALS: Wallpaper, paste, water, overlap adhesive

1 At an internal corner, match the pattern and brush out the paper as usual, but only go as far as the corner crease. Allow the paper that has folded around the corner to loosely stick to the unpapered wall. This will make it easier to work down the length, pushing the paper into the corner junction.

2 Use the scissors to make a diagonal cut directly into the three-way junction where the wall, ceiling and corner all meet. The cut should extend as far as the actual corner itself. Make a similar cut at ground level into the junction at the skirting board and the corner.

3 Use a craft knife to make a vertical cut from ceiling to floor allowing a 1–2 cm (¼–½in) overlap of paper on to the unpapered wall. It may be easier to begin and end this vertical cut using scissors.

4 Remove the offcut and place it temporarily on the unpapered wall. Return to the other part, to trim the top and bottom, and to make sure that the paper is firmly stuck down in the corner junction.

5 Move the offcut section to overlap the hung section of paper along the entire length of the corner, matching the pattern as closely as possible. With vinyl coverings especially it may be necessary to use a stronger adhesive to bond the corner overlap. In such cases, pull back the paper edge along the vertical corner and apply some overlap adhesive, either straight from the tube or using a fitch. Then firmly push the paper back into its proper position.

6 To hang the second strip it is essential to use a spirit level in order to make sure you are starting the next wall with a completely vertical edge. When the position is correct, trim the top and bottom as usual. Finally, sponge down thoroughly as any overlap will always leave paste on the surface.

CHECKING THE HORIZONTAL

With some straight-match papers it may also be necessary to use a spirit level across the corner to check the horizontal line.

External corners

It is rare to find a completely square edge on an external corner. Therefore, when papering around them, it is often necessary to realign the paper to the vertical. This may be done by simply overlapping the new length on to the previous one. However, this often produces an untidy finish.

As described under Lining, manufacturing a butt join is the most appropriate technique (see pages 42–43). Having a pattern to match makes the process a little more complicated than with lining paper, but by using the following steps a professional result can be achieved.

TOOLS: Pasting table, 2 buckets, sponge, pasting brush, paper-hanging brush, wallpaper trough (if needed), step-ladder, tape measure, scissors, craft knife, steel rule, seam roller, spirit level

MATERIALS: Wallpaper, paste, water

1 When approaching an external corner, hang the paper as usual and bend the excess around the corner using the paper-hanging brush to expel bubbles and ensure good adhesion along the corner edge. Allow the section of paper which has gone around the corner to loosely attach itself in the central area of the wall. Do not apply too much pressure to the paper above or below this point as you risk tearing the paper at ceiling or ground level.

2 Using scissors, make a diagonal cut precisely into the skirting–corner junction and then at the ceiling–corner junction. It will now be easier to smooth out both sections of the length on either side of the corner.

3 Trim the top and bottom and check there are no bubbles along the corner. If the new starting edge is completely vertical, you may continue to hang the next length. However, in many cases the paper edge will be off the vertical and so some adjustment is needed. Therefore it is necessary to follows steps 4 to 8 (see right).

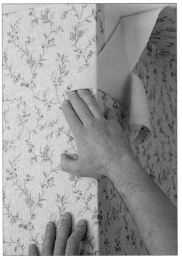

5 Hang a new length of wallpaper, covering the trimmed overlap with the edge of the new piece. However, this rough join will be quite obvious to the naked eye and risks spoiling the neatness of the finished result. The best way of solving this is to move the new length of wallpaper into such a position that although it overlaps the previous length of paper, you are also matching the pattern exactly. The width of the design will obviously affect the degree to which you may have to overlap the two lengths. Once positioned, make sure the new length is level, making a small compromise with the pattern match if necessary. Trim the new length top and bottom, as usual.

4 Use a craft knife to trim the paper back to the corner leaving a 4cm (1½in) overlap around the corner.

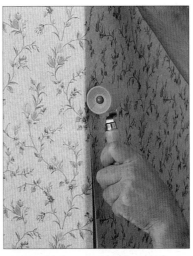

6 Place a steel rule vertically on the corner, 2cm (¾in) from the edge and use a craft knife to cut through the two lengths of overlapping paper. Move the straight edge and repeat the process, so continuing the cut from ceiling to skirting.

7 Carefully pull back this cut edge on the overlapping piece of wallpaper, and gently remove the two strips of excess paper that were stuck on top of each other. Take care not to damage the top edge, so that it makes a neat join when replaced.

8 Push the edge back together using a paper-hanging brush. You will have a perfect butt join with the pattern still matching. A seam roller can be useful here to make sure of a totally flat join. Finally, use a clean, damp sponge to clean off excess paste.

Doors and obstacles

Papering around any obstacle that stands out from the wall, such as a door, window or fireplace, calls for skilful trimming in order to obtain a neat finish.

Part of the technique involves knowing the directions in which to make the cuts, but for a completely successful finish, a sharp craft knife is absolutely vital. To keep the knife's edge sharp it is essential to keep the blade free from wallpaper paste and to change it at regular intervals.

TOOLS: Pasting table, 2 buckets, sponge, pasting brush, paper-hanging brush, wallpaper trough (if needed), step-ladder, scissors, craft knife

MATERIALS: Wallpaper, paste, water, clean cloth

FIREPLACE

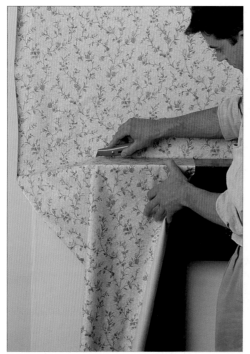

1 Allow the paper to flap over the top of the fireplace and push the paper into the wall–mantlepiece junction with the paper-hanging brush. Use a craft knife to cut from the top corner of the fireplace along the creased edge.

2 Put a finger on the corner of the cut and pick up the paper flap, gently moulding it into the angles with the paper-hanging brush. Make a series of right-angled cuts into the finely detailed areas.

3 Carefully trim each of the small flaps using a craft knife, taking care not to damage or scratch the mouldings underneath the paper.

4 Smooth the paper into its final position. Remove any excess paste from the fireplace to avoid discolouring the decorated surface.

DOOR

1 When the papering arrives at the door, match the pattern at a high level and then allow the remainder of the length to fall loosely over the door architrave. Using the paper-hanging brush, push the paper firmly into the top of the architrave.

2 Use your finger to mark the point where the corner of the architrave meets the wall, and using the scissors, make a diagonal cut towards this point. As you near the final point, move your finger back slightly to take the weight of the paper.

3 As you work down the length, continue to match the pattern with the previous length of paper and then push the vertical overlap of paper firmly into the junction of the wall and the door architrave. Make sure that during this process you do not allow the whole length to move, thus breaking the pattern match with the previous piece of paper.

4 Trim the two flaps with a craft knife. Use the blade at a 45-degree angle to the wall surface, keeping as steady a hand as possible. By making the cut slightly on to the architrave surface you will find it easier to keep a straight line as many junctions between wood and plaster are often uneven. Remember to wipe the excess paste off the woodwork immediately.

Recessed windows

Tackling a recessed window combines many of the techniques already described in this chapter. However, particular attention must be given to the order of applying the paper. It is also vital to make sure that all edges are stuck down firmly as, of all areas in the home, this is where wallpaper can be subjected to condensation problems or a wide range of temperatures.

Although a great deal of care is required to produce a neat finish around such an obstacle, beginners may take comfort in the fact that most of the joins needed will often be obscured by curtains or rails.

TOOLS: Pasting table, 2 buckets, sponge, pasting brush, paper-hanging brush, wallpaper trough (if needed), step-ladder, tape measure, scissors, craft knife, steel rule, seam roller

MATERIALS: Wallpaper, paste, water

1 When the papering arrives at the window, pattern match the length as normal and allow the paper to drop over the window recess. Make sure the area of wallpaper to the top and side of the recess is firmly stuck down in position.

2 Make two horizontal cuts back to the corners. Cut at the bottom using the window sill as a guide, then at the top, along the recess edge. Do not allow the paper to tear under its own weight. Attach the flap loosely to the wall of the recess.

3 Use the scissors to make a series of right-angled cuts into the profile of the bottom corner of the sill. This will then allow the paper to be moulded around and under the sill so that the bottom half of the length can be positioned and trimmed.

4 You may now use the same technique as described for external corners on pages 68–69 to bend the flap of paper around and into the recess. Push the paper firmly into the junction between the wall and the window frame and trim all areas as usual.

5 Cut the next length to extend from the ceiling around the top of the recess to the top of the frame. Hang it overlapping the previous length, matching the pattern. Mark the recess corner with your finger and make a diagonal cut to this point.

6 Now make a manufactured butt join. Use a steel rule and a craft knife to cut a diagonal line through the area where the two pieces overlap. Make sure the line goes through the busiest part of the pattern to disguise the join as much as possible.

7 Peel back the paper and discard the top section of the first length. Remove the bottom section of the new length, and push the pieces back together to produce a perfect butt join.

8 Bend the remaining flap around the top recess holding the paper at the recess corner to avoid tearing. Notice that in step 5 a diagonal cut was made. This is to enable you to tuck a small overlap of this section behind the flap on the side recess wall, thus producing a neat finish. Finally, trim and clean all areas with a damp sponge. Complete the rest of the window in the same way.

Stairwells

The primary concern when working in stairwells is safety. To provide a stable platform it is possible to hire scaffold towers which are designed to be erected in stairwells, but you can build your own working platform with a little ingenuity. Make sure that any planks used are rigid enough to bear your weight, and tie them to the ladders with rope.

As you are working with long lengths of paper, it is much easier to complete the job with two people.

TOOLS: Ladders, planks, rope, paper-hanging equipment, spirit level, tape measure, scissors, craft knife

MATERIALS: Wallpaper, paste, water, masking tape, stockinette roll

Making a platform

Secure planks to the step-ladder and ladder(s) with rope to avoid any slippage.

Make sure that the plank is sturdy; scaffolding planks are the best for this purpose. If you are bridging a gap of 1.5m (5ft) or more, tie two planks together, one on top of each other, for extra strength.

For spans that are longer than 2.4–3m (8–10ft) extra support should be used in the middle of the plank. Combination ladders, where one side can be made longer than the other, are excellent for setting up on steps.

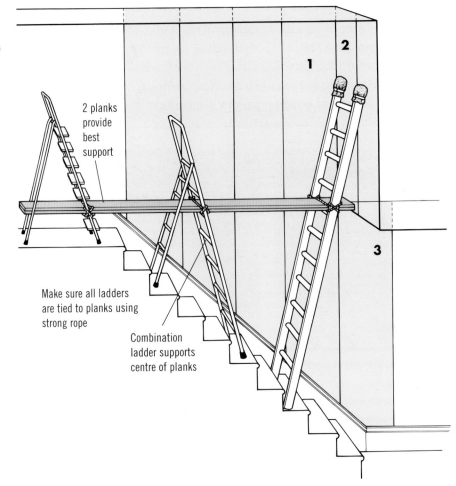

2 planks provide best support

1

2

3

Make sure all ladders are tied to planks using strong rope

Combination ladder supports centre of planks

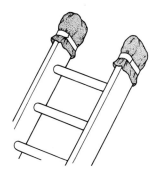

Protecting the wall

To avoid damaging new paper or a bare surface, pad the ends of the ladder. Use some stockinette roll or any soft cloth, held in place with masking tape.

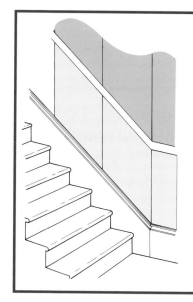

Divided walls

The bottom levels of paper are the most likely to be damaged and receive the most physical abuse. By using two papers or even painting the lower section of wall, you can avoid having to redecorate the entire hallway and can tackle just the bottom section instead.

Order of work

Start hanging the paper with the longest length. It is important to make sure that your first length is perfectly vertical as a minute stray from vertical at the top is hugely increased by the time you reach the bottom of the length. To find the vertical, it may help to use a plumb line.

By working up the stairs as illustrated right, measuring subsequent lengths is made much more straightforward than if you worked down the stairs.

Once you have completed all the lengths (to the left of point 1, in the diagram left), and on the opposite wall, if required, it is possible to then dismantle the platform, leaving just the long ladder in order to hang the lengths from point 2 (see left).

As illustrated above, padding on the ends of the ladder is vital to prevent damaging the wallpaper.

Finally, remove the ladder and continue from point 3 to finish the other walls downstairs. Continue papering on the upper floor, if required.

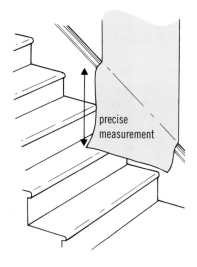

precise measurement

Papering up stairs

The shape of walls above staircases can waste a great deal of paper. It is easy to make measuring mistakes if you work down the stairs as you can only make a rough measurement as to where the paper end will drop. To avoid expensive mistakes it is much easier to work from the longest length back up the stairs, as described and illustrated left.

PATTERN OF PAPER

Certain patterns have particular effects in stairwells. Stripes will appear to raise the height of the walls. A busy pattern, which by nature usually matches well, will reduce the risk of pattern-drop problems or unavoidable overlaps on such a wide, open area.

Archways

Wallpapering around a curved arch is not as daunting as it may first appear. Clearly, pattern matching is somewhat complicated, so it is not advisable to use papers where a distinct pattern match is crucial. Also avoid vertical stripes, as the curve of the arch will disturb the vertical nature of the pattern.

Busy or floral wallpaper patterns are ideal for arches as the naked eye will be too busy admiring the overall effect of the curved shape, rather than noticing any imperfections in the joins or corners.

TOOLS: Pasting table, 2 buckets, sponge, pasting brush, paper-hanging brush, wallpaper trough (if needed), step-ladder, craft knife, scissors, tape measure, fitch

MATERIALS: Wallpaper, paste, water, overlap adhesive

1 Allow the first length to hang over the arch. Pattern match it to the preceding length as usual, and make sure the paper is firmly positioned around the top and side of the arch.

2 Use scissors to trim the section of paper hanging in the arch, cutting back to 2.5cm (1in) from the edge of the arch. Support the paper to ensure an accurate cut.

3 Working just around the curved part of the arch, use the scissors to make a series of cuts at right-angles to the edge. They should be spaced at intervals of about 1cm (½in).

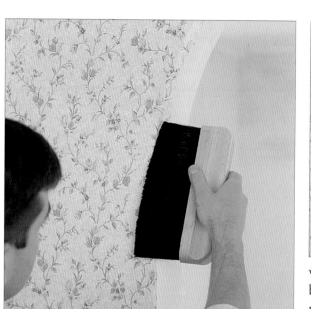

4 Brush down the miniature flaps around the curve, and the remainder of the overlap on the vertical edge of the arch. Hang the next lengths of paper on the flat wall above the arch, using the same technique to cope with the curve.

5 Before completing the inside of the arch, paper the flat wall on the other side of the arch, if required. For the curved surface, cut a strip of paper 3cm (1¼in) wider than the width of the arch. With a free match pattern it may be possible to use one length of paper going around the whole arch. However, where there is a definite 'right way up' for the paper, you will need two lengths (that join at the highest point) to avoid the pattern going upside down on one side. Line up the manufactured edge of the measured length with the edge of the arch in order to keep a vertical guideline. Only trim initially at skirting level.

6 With a sharp craft knife, trim the paper on the arch edge by holding the flat blade of the craft knife up against the edge of the arch and steadily cutting downwards. Hang the second length on the other side of the arch, if necessary, using the same technique. Where these two lengths meet at the top of the arch, manufacture a butt join to avoid an overlap; use a steel rule as shown on pages 72–73.

7 Because of the unavoidable overlaps produced when papering an arch, it may be necessary to use overlap adhesive to stick down troublesome areas. Use a fitch to apply it and remember to sponge off any excess adhesive.

Wall-mounted fittings

It is difficult to paper around wall-mounted fittings such as lights and central-heating radiators, and it is usually easier to remove them. However, removing a radiator may be problematic due to old pipework and connections that have seized up.

Wall lights should be easy to take down, but if they prove difficult to move, be careful to keep paste off brass and other fittings as it will quickly tarnish them.

For guidelines on how to trim around electrical wall sockets and switches, see pages 48–49.

TOOLS: Pasting table, 2 buckets, sponge, pasting brush, paper-hanging brush, wallpaper trough (if needed), step-ladder, tape measure, craft knife, scissors, pencil, radiator roller, screwdriver

MATERIALS: Wallpaper, paste, water, electrical insulating tape

RADIATORS

1 Allow the paper to fall over the top of the radiator, making sure that the top section of the length is correctly joined with the previously hung piece. Pull the paper back slightly and using a pencil, mark the location of the supporting bracket.

2 Make a vertical cut with scissors from the bottom of the paper, just up to the pencil mark. Paste from the paper will inevitably get on the radiator, but it can be wiped off when you have finished fixing the paper to the wall behind.

3 Using a radiator roller, push the paper into position on either side of the supporting bracket. Trim the paper below the radiator, as usual, and wipe off any excess paste from all surfaces. Repeat steps 1–3 when papering around the other bracket.

LIGHT FITTINGS

1 Turn off the electricity supply at the mains or consumer unit. Unscrew the wall-mounted fitting, taking care to support its weight until it is free of the wall.

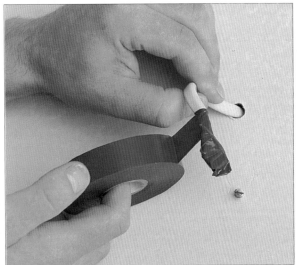

2 Using electrical insulating tape, cover the exposed wires. Replace the supporting screws in the wall. It may be helpful to draw a diagram of the wire layout to assist you when replacing the fitting.

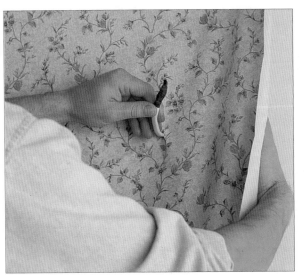

3 Allow the paper to fall over the area. Mark the position where the wire protrudes from the wall, using a pencil. With scissors, make a small cut in the paper on this mark, then carefully thread the wire through the hole.

4 Using a paper-hanging brush, smooth out the paper, allowing the wall screws to break through the paper surface. Trim the rest of the paper as necessary. Allow the paper to dry out completely before replacing the fitting.

Ceilings

The technique used to wallpaper a ceiling is similar to that discussed under Lining (pages 36–37) except that pattern considerations make it necessary to ensure that the paper is squared up correctly on the ceiling. Again, it is much easier to paper a ceiling with two people, but it is still perfectly possible to tackle it on your own provided you take your time and take care, especially when applying the first length.

When using an embossed paper on ceilings or walls, as illustrated here, take care not to apply too much pressure to the paper surface as you may flatten the relief.

TOOLS: Trestles, planks, pasting table, 2 buckets, sponge, pasting brush, paper-hanging brush, wallpaper trough (if needed), scissors, tape measure, chalk line, hammer, craft knife

MATERIALS: Wallpaper, paste, water, 2 nails, chalk

1 Decide on the direction in which to hang the lengths, and set up planks and trestles. Measure out from the side wall the exact width of the paper, minus a 2.5cm (1in) overlap on to the wall. Do this for both ends of the first length. This allows for any ceiling–wall junction unevenness and for trimming.

2 A chalk line, snapped against the ceiling, is ideal for providing a long, straight guideline for hanging the first length accurately. At each end of the measured width, hammer a small nail into the ceiling. Do not knock the nails in too far or removal will be difficult.

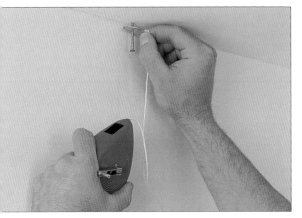

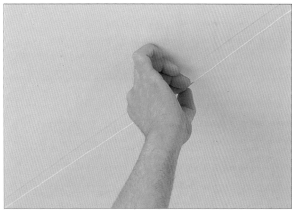

3 Apply some ordinary coloured chalk to a chalk line. If you do not have a proper chalk line, some household string will do as long as the chalk dust loosely bonds with the string. Attach the line to the nails. Make sure that the line is taut.

4 Go to the centre of the plank, pull the line down approximately 5–10cm (2–4in) from the ceiling and then release it. This snapping action leaves a straight chalk line on the ceiling. Remove the line and nails.

5 Now that the guideline is in place, begin papering at the junction between the wall and the ceiling using the chalk guideline to position the edge of the first length precisely. This should give the planned 2.5cm (1in) overlap on to the wall as measured in step 1.

6 Use the paper-hanging brush to brush out bubbles and push the paper into the wall–ceiling junction. See pages 36–37 under Lining for further instructions on trimming. You will find that once this first length is in position, subsequent lengths are far less time consuming.

Borders

The appearance of a room can be dramatically changed by a border, whether applied over wallpaper or a painted surface. At whatever height you choose to hang the border it is important to ensure that it is level or it may give an unbalanced effect to the rest of your decoration. Border adhesive tends to dry very quickly so always tackle one wall at a time and never attempt to go around the entire room with one length.

TOOLS: Pasting table, bucket, sponge, small pasting brush, paper-hanging brush, spirit level, scissors, tape measure, pencil

MATERIALS: Border, border adhesive, water

1 Measure from the top of the skirting up to the height at which you want the top or bottom of the border to hang and make a mark with a pencil. From this mark use a spirit level to draw a guideline right around the room. However, do not press too hard with the pencil or the line may show through the border once it is hung.

2 Measure the width of the first wall, adding a 5cm (2in) overlap at each end. Cut this length and using a small brush add the border adhesive to the reverse side. Concertina the border (see pages 56–57) and leave it to soak for the required time.

3 Starting in one corner of the first wall, apply the border to the wall. Let the 5cm (2in) overlap go around the corner and on to the adjacent wall. The border edge should follow the pencil line, but slightly overlapping it so that the pencil marks will not be visible once the border is hung.

SELF-ADHESIVE BORDERS
These are easy to use, as
you simply peel away the
backing paper. They
obviously produce less mess
but it is difficult to adjust
the position of some once
they are stuck down.

4 Continue along to the other
corner, brushing out any air
bubbles and making sure that the
border is perfectly level. Again,
allow the 5cm (2in) overlap to go
round the corner.

5 In both corners, use scissors
to trim the paper back to
leave a 5mm (¼in) overlap on to
the adjacent wall. Then sponge
down the entire length to remove
any excess adhesive.

6 Pattern
match the
end of the next
piece of dry
border to the
corner you
have just
finished
hanging. Then
roll out the dry
border along
the length of
the wall, to
find out the
length you
need, and again add a single 5cm (2in) overlap (not
10cm (4in) as in step 2). Paste up the new length
and apply to the wall as before. Take care to match
the pattern in the corner by allowing the new
length to overlap on top of the old length. Once
positioned correctly, score down the crease of the
corner using scissors, peel back the new length and
cut directly along the creased line.

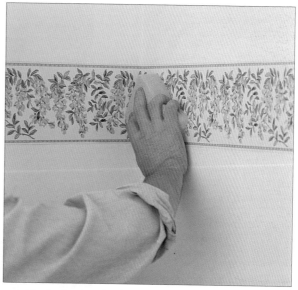

7 Push the border back into position using a
sponge to remove excess adhesive. The small
overlap that was left on the previous length reduces
any danger of a line or gap appearing in the corner,
especially if the corner junction is not square. The
overlap therefore improves the finish and is
practically invisible. Continue to hang the rest of
the border using the same techniques.

Divides and mitring

Borders can be hung to provide a decorative divide between different wallpapers; in a rectangle to produce shapes like panelling; or to highlight the features of a room, such as framing a window. To achieve a neat finish it is necessary to join the horizontal and vertical lengths with a mitred join. Because you will not be able to pattern match the border exactly on each join, choose the border carefully; busy florals tend to hide any inconsistencies in pattern match better than symmetric designs.

TOOLS: Pasting table, bucket, sponge, small pasting brush, paper-hanging brush, step-ladder, scissors, tape measure, pencil, craft knife, steel rule, spirit level

MATERIALS: Border, border adhesive, water

BORDER DIVIDES

2 Using the level of the pencil line on the wall as a guide cut through the overlapping paper. Remove the excess strips, creating a manufactured butt join. (This is a similar technique to that shown on pages 68–69).

3 Hang the border using the technique described on pages 82–83. If you are lucky the pattern of the wallpaper will give you a ready-made level guideline to follow, eliminating the need to make a pencil line.

1 Using a border to separate two different wallpapers can be very effective. Before hanging the wallpaper make a pencil line on the wall at the height where the centre of the border is to hang. Hang the two papers at the same time with each overlapping the pencil line by 5cm (2in).

CREATING WALL PANELS WITH A MITRED FRAME

For wall panels the first, top measurement should be exactly the length of the top side of the panel required. Then continue to make precise measurements for the other three sides. This will ensure consistency with the other panels you apply. However, when applying a single frame the top horizontal guideline is all that is needed.

MITRED FRAME

1 Use a pencil and spirit level to make a horizontal guideline above the window to the correct width of the finished border. Cut the first length of border 5cm (2in) longer than the exact length required. Paste the border as described on pages 82–83 and apply to the wall following the pencil guideline. Make sure that there is an equal overlap of border on each side of the frame.

2 Cut the first vertical length, again 5cm (2in) longer than the height required. Paste it and hang it on the wall using the spirit level to maintain an exact vertical line. The overlap that has been allowed is useful in order to try and adjust the pattern so that you will be cutting through the busiest part of the design in step 3, making the join less visible.

3 Hold a steel rule at a 45-degree angle from the external to the internal corner of the border frame. Cut through the two lengths of border using a craft knife.

4 Peel back the two long strips of border and remove the excess flaps that are stuck to the wall. Brush the paper back into position creating a perfect mitred join.

5 Hang the second vertical length of border and then last, the bottom horizontal length. Be sure to keep removing excess adhesive from all surfaces with a clean damp sponge.

Problems and faults 1

Occasionally, after paper-hanging has been completed, a variety of problems can occur with the finish. Some of these may be rectified relatively easily, but in other cases you may have to strip and re-hang all the paper in the spoilt area. The next four pages provide solutions for the most common wallpaper problems.

TOOLS: Bucket, sponge, paper-hanging brush, fitch, craft knife, seam roller

MATERIALS: Water, overlap adhesive, felt-tip pen

OVERLAPPING OR LIFTING SEAMS

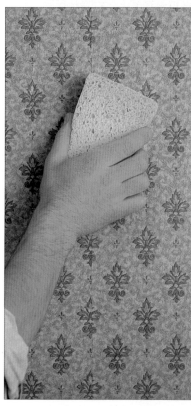

1 Small overlaps can occur when papering. The paper may not form a strong bond at the overlap, especially with vinyl papers. As a result, the edge lifts away from the wall surface.

2 Use a fitch to apply some overlap adhesive. If the overlap is too small to allow access with a fitch, lever the overlap away from the wall surface with the blunt edge of a craft knife.

3 Smooth the paper back into position with a damp sponge, removing any excess adhesive in the process. A seam roller may also be used to push the paper back down on to the wall.

BUBBLING PAPER

1 Some bubbles in the paper surface are often excess wet paste and will disappear during the drying process. You can test this by gently pressing down on the bubble to feel for the paste. However, once the paper has dried out completely, any bubbles left are just trapped air and will not disappear of their own accord.

Normally, these have been caused by not allowing the paper to soak for enough time before application, or because the wall surface below was poorly prepared and so the paper has not stuck to the wall.

2 If there are only a few bubbles, pierce each bubble with a craft knife and use a fitch to apply some paste or overlap adhesive to the wall. Stick the paper back and sponge off any excess adhesive.

If the problem is extensive, strip the paper off, prepare the wall thoroughly and remember to allow the paper to soak for the required time before reapplying it.

CREASES

Caused by poor technique or when stretching paper around an external corner that is not square. Remedy in a similar way to bubbling paper. If the problem is extensive, strip and re-hang the paper.

WHITE SEAMS

1 Commonly caused by poor butt joining during application, or shrinkage while the paper was drying out. This is especially found in new houses where complete drying out and the settling process are not finished. Similarly, old houses can have the same problem when they have had new central heating installed.

2 It is always advisable to allow the structure of a new house to settle – for about a year – before applying wallpaper. In minor instances, use a felt-tip pen or crayon of a similar colour to the base colour of the paper, and carefully run down the affected seams. Some paper manufacturers provide special felt tips for exactly this purpose.

Problems and faults 2

Most problems with wallpapering occur because of poor technique or hasty preparation, rather than faults with the paper itself. Always remember to take your time when applying wallpaper as some mistakes can only be rectified by stripping the entire area and starting again. As well as being frustrating, this can be very costly.

TOOLS: Bucket, sponge, paper-hanging brush, fitch, craft knife, seam roller

MATERIALS: Water, overlap adhesive

DAMP STAINS

Before panicking about damp stains, allow the paper to dry out completely. With some heavy papers, this may take days. If any patches still do not disappear, strip the paper and treat the damp problem in the wall underneath (see pages 28–29).

SAGGING PAPER

Caused by too much pressure being applied with the paper-hanging brush during application, so that it stretches and creases the wet, pliable wallpaper. If the effect is too noticeable, stripping and repapering will be necessary.

POOR PATTERN MATCH

Normally caused by poor application, in which case the only solution is to strip the paper and start again. Sometimes there is a variation in the degree to which the pattern matches along a seam. More tolerance to this sort of imperfection is necessary if the paper is hand printed. In some cases, the paper may be from a faulty batch, so you should always check how well the pattern matches at the early stages of preparation. (See pages 52, 54–55 and 64–65.)

STAINED SEAMS OR PASTE ON PAPER

If paste has dried on the surface of the paper this will often show, spoiling the decorative finish (especially on some matt wallpapers). This is caused by not wiping wet paste from the surface during paper hanging. If the paper is washable try removing the paste with a sponge and a solution of mild detergent. Similar to this is shiny seams where the joins have been over brushed during application resulting in a polished effect. There is no remedy, so be less vigorous when you next hang wallpaper.

TORN PAPER

Caused by accidentally snagging the paper on something. A tear often looks devastating, but by carefully applying some overlap adhesive and pushing the paper back into place, most tears become invisible to the naked eye.

FLATTENED RELIEF

Caused by applying too much pressure, normally on embossed papers, when hanging. Never use a seam roller on such papers. Small areas should not be too noticeable; larger areas may need stripping and repapering.

Cleaning up

Once papering has been completed, it is essential to spend time cleaning equipment and clearing up. It would be irritating to find stiff brushes, grimy buckets and paste-covered scissors when next starting a decorating job. You would immediately regret not clearing up properly last time, and may have to buy some new equipment.

Unused rolls of paper should be stored in a dry place, with part-used rolls bound with tape to prevent them unrolling and getting damaged.

TOOLS: Sponge, bucket with lid, nail

MATERIALS: Detergent, clean cloth, water

1 Wash the paper-hanging brush under warm running water using household detergent to remove any dry paste. Rinse thoroughly and allow to dry before storing. To clean the pasting brush, remove as much excess paste as possible from the bristles. Then wash, rinse and dry in the same way.

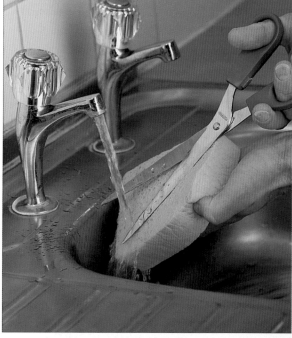

2 Rinse the paper-hanging scissors in warm water under the tap, sponging off any dry paste which would otherwise blunt the cutting edges. Make sure to thoroughly dry every part of the scissors with a clean cloth, to prevent any possibility of corrosion.

3 If you have overestimated the amount of paste required for the job, and are likely to need more in the near future, it can be stored for a few weeks in an airtight container.

4 Wipe the table with clean water and a sponge, paying particular attention to the edges where paste generally collects. Only fold up the table to store when it is completely dry.

5 It is important to seal a partly used tube of flexible filler so that it does not dry out and become impossible to use again. Place a nail in the end of the nozzle.

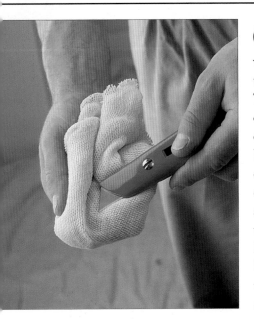

6 Before putting away a craft knife, it should be carefully wiped clean with a damp cloth to remove all traces of paste. Then dry it thoroughly. For obvious safety reasons, dispose of old blades – even if they are blunt – by placing them in a container such as an empty paint can. Make sure the can is sealed securely before putting it out with the rest of the rubbish. Metal objects such as these blades are recyclable, an option which should always be considered.

PASTE DISPOSAL
Most wallpaper paste contains fungicide and so is not biodegradable. Therefore, paste should never be tipped down a drain, as it may pollute nearby streams and water tables. Put it in a container that can be sealed before throwing it out.

Glossary

Architrave
Decorative moulding surrounding a door or window which covers the join between the frame and the wall.

Batten
A length of straight wood, used as a guideline.

Border
A narrow, decorative band of wallpaper.

Butt join
A join where two edges of wallpaper or lining paper meet exactly, but do not overlap.

Ceiling rose
An electrical fitting found on ceilings through which a lighting pendant hangs.

Centralisation
The process of centring the dominant part of the pattern in a wallpaper on a focal point in a room, such as the middle of a chimney breast.

Chalk line
A length of string covered in chalk dust, pulled tight and snapped against a surface to leave a straight guideline.

Concertina
Wallpaper or lining paper that has been folded into manageable lengths, usually after pasting.

Double lining
Two layers of lining paper, used to achieve a smooth finish on a rough surface.

External corner
A corner where two walls meet, that sticks out into the room.

Flush
Term used to describe two level, adjacent surfaces.

Fungicide
A chemical that kills mould.

Internal corner
A corner where two walls meet, that does not stick out into the room.

Key
A slightly rough surface that has been sanded to provide a bond for paint or paper.

Lining paper
Plain paper that gives a smooth surface on walls and ceilings prior to painting or hanging wall coverings.

Manufactured butt join
The process of overlapping wall coverings, cutting through both layers of paper and removing the excess strips to create a flush butt join.

Mitre
An angled cut, made when joining two lengths of border in order to change direction. It is usually a 45-degree cut used to form a 90-degree corner.

Paste-the-wall paper
Paper that is applied dry to a wall which has had paste applied to it directly.

Pattern drop
The misalignment of a pattern match.

Pattern repeat
The length over which a pattern repeats itself on a length of wallpaper.

Plumb line
Length of string to which a weight is attached, giving a vertical guideline.

Proud
Protruding slightly from the surrounding surface.

Ready-pasted paper
Paper that has had paste coated on it when it was made. The paste is reactivated by soaking the paper in water before it is hung.

Recessed window
A window that is flush with the external wall thus creating a recess inside a room.

Seam roller
A small, narrow plastic, felt or wooden roller used to roll gently along wallpaper seams to ensure good adhesion.

Size
A stabilising compound applied to porous surfaces to seal them before paper hanging.

Soaking
Allowing a period of time for the the wallpaper paste to soak into the paper.

Stripping
Removal of old wallpaper from a wall.

Wall-ceiling junction
The corner where a wall meets the ceiling.

Wallpaper trough
A specially shaped container designed to hold water, for the purpose of soaking ready-pasted papers.

Index

*The authors and publisher would like to thank the
following for their assistance in producing this book:*

Akzo Nobel Decorative Coatings, Darwin, Lancashire
Crossley's, Castle Cary, Somerset
Dave Marsh Hardware, Castle Cary, Somerset
Kath Kidston Wallpaper, London
McDougall Rose Decorating Merchants, Altrincham, Cheshire
Nectar Imports, Mere, Wiltshire
Nostalgia Furniture (Bruton Cast Iron Ltd), Bruton, Somerset
Ramm, Son & Crocker Ltd, High Wycombe, Buckinghamshire
Wemyss Houlès Trimmings, London

Editor: Margot Richardson
Designers: Hilary Prosser and John Round

Managing Editor: Miranda Spicer
Art Director: Martin Lovelock

Photography: James Merrell
Cut-outs: Polly Wreford, Tim Ridley

'Ideas and Choices' stylist: Julia Barnard
Illustrator: David Eaton

Production Manager: Kevin Perrett
Set Builder: Nigel Tate

Julian Cassell and Peter Parham have asserted their
right to be identified as the authors of this work.

First published 1996

Text, photographs and illustrations
© Haynes Publishing 1996

Published by: Haynes Publishing
Sparkford, Nr Yeovil, Somerset BA22 7JJ

British Library Cataloguing-in-Publication Data:
A catalogue record for this book is available from
the British Library.

ISBN 1 85960 106 5

Printed in France by
Imprimerie Pollina, 85400 Luçon - n° 68975 - B